Amelia Earhart was born in Atchison, Kansas, in 1898. In *The Fun of It* she describes her childhood and education, and her work as nurse, teacher and social worker before she discovered the overwhelming fascination of airplanes and made flying her life's work.

In 1931, already a respected aviator, she married George Palmer Putnam, on the conditions that they would separate if either was unhappy at the end of one year, and that they would be equally free to pursue their own careers, wherever they might lead. Amelia Earhart continued to accept new challenges and new risks. Before one dangerous flight she wrote her husband: "I want to do it because I want to do it. Women must try to do things as men have tried. When they fail, their failure must be but a challenge to others."

In 1937 she embarked with navigator Fred Noonan on an around-the-world flight that ended when her plane was lost in the South Pacific. Their fate has remained a mystery.

Amelia Earhart was aviation editor for *Cosmopolitan* from 1928 to 1930. Her other books are *20 Hrs. 40 Min.* (1928) and *Last Flight* (1937) compiled by G.P. Putnam.

A.E.

Amelia Earhart

The Fun of It

Random Records of My Own Flying
And of Women in Aviation

Academy
Chicago
Publishers

Academy Chicago Publishers
An imprint of Chicago Review Press Incorporated
814 North Franklin Street
Chicago, Illinois 60610

First Academy Chicago edition 1977
ISBN 978-0-91586-455-3

Printed in the United States of America

Cover design: Sarah Olson

Library of Congress Cataloging-in-Publication data
Earhart, Amelia, 1898–1937.
     The fun of it.
Reprint of the ed. published by Harcourt Brace, New York
     1. Earhart, Amelia, 1898–1937.
     2. Women in aeronautics [1. Earhart, Amelia, 1898–1937.
2. Air pilots. 3. Women in aeronautics]
     I. Title.
  TL540.E3A3   1977
  629.13'092.4 — [B] [92] 77-16052
  ISBN-10: 0-915864-55-X
  ISBN-13: 978-0-915864-55-3

To the
Ninety Nines

CONTENTS

LIST OF ILLUSTRATIONS

The Fun of It

THE FUN OF IT

GROWING UP HERE AND THERE

WHENEVER anyone asks me about my work in aviation I know that sooner or later I shall hear, "And, of course, you were mechanical when you were a girl, weren't you?" As a matter of fact, in a small way, I was—witness the trap I made to catch the chickens that strayed into our yard. My girlhood was much like that of many another American girl who was growing up at the time I was, with just the kind of fun and good times we all had then.

Looking back now, however, I can see certain threads in what I did that were fully as important in leading me to aviation as being mechanical perhaps was. There is the thread of my father's being a railroad man and the many trips we had together —by which I discovered the fascination of new people and new places. There is the thread of liking all kinds of sports and games and of not being afraid to try those that some of my elders in those days looked upon as being only for boys. There is the thread of liking to experiment—perhaps this thread is the same as the one I have just mentioned —and of the something inside me that has always liked to try new things. There they all are, weaving in and out and here and there through the years before aviation and I got together.

But to begin at the beginning.

Among the best stories my mother told were those of her own girlhood. My sister and I always spoke of that mysterious and far away period as "thousands of years ago when Mother was little". Looking back on my own infant days I seem to feel a new significance in that childish quotation. So I think I'll begin this sketchy history of me by using it.

Well, then, thousands of years ago, I was born in Atchison, Kansas. My parents did not live there at the time, but my grandparents did. My grandfather was a judge of the district court, though he had retired from that office and others he held long before he became a relative of mine. My grandmother was a Philadelphian, having come out from that city after the war. Her family were Quakers, and she had lived within sight of old Christ Church in a house which stands today. I think inside she never quite got used to the west, for now and then something came popping out which made me feel Philadelphia must be quite superior to Atchison (this point, of course, has never been proved).

She arrived when Kansas was really wild. Great piles of buffalo bones lined the newly built railroad tracks when *she* came and Indians in blankets were always to be seen in the town. I remember her telling me of their crowding about her when, as a young housewife, she went to market. They lifted the lid of her basket and peered within, and felt the fabric of her dress, until she was quite terrified, mistaking their native curiosity for some kind of sinister threats.

There were no Indians around when I arrived, though I hoped for many a day some would turn up. And the nearest I got to buffaloes was the discovery of an old fur robe rotting away in the barn. Truly the Kansas I knew had lost some of its woolliness.

Before I return to my beginnings, I should mention that I had two more grandparents. My father's father was a Lutheran minister, he and his wife both coming from Pennsylvania. I barely remember him as a tall, slight man with very thin hands, and she was not living when I was born.

I went to school in Atchison in a private college preparatory until I was ready for high school. I was named for my grandmother and was lent her for company during the winter months. I am sure I was a horrid little girl, and I do not see how she put up with me, even part time. Like many horrid children, I loved school, though I never qualified as teacher's pet. Perhaps the fact that I was exceedingly fond of reading made me endurable. With a large library to browse in, I spent many hours not bothering anyone, after I once learned to read. Scott, Dickens, George Eliot, Thackeray, Harper's Magazine for Young People, and The

Youth's Companion of a generation past fell before my onslaught, as well as forgotten books like Dr. Syntax. On the crowded shelves I also found waiting for me the so-called children's books of fifty years ago, where very good little boys and girls always emerged triumphant over very bad little boys and girls.

I go back now to few of the books I read as a child since without a feeling of disappointment. Whether this is in the books, or in me, I do not know. I suppose mine is a repetition of the experience of the elderly gentleman who returned to his native country after many years abroad to taste the cherries he was so fond of as a boy. Of course, he found that they were no better than those he had been eating regularly in other parts of the world. And everyone over thirty understands this. Note: This point is not important enough to wish to be thirty to understand.

Books have meant much to me. Not only did I myself read considerably, but Mother read aloud to my sister and me, early and late. So fundamental became the habit that on occasions when we girls had to do housework, instead of both pitching in and doing it together, one was selected to read aloud and the other to work.

At one time I thought that my father must have read everything and, of course, therefore, knew everything. He could define the hardest words as well as the dictionary and we used to try to trip him and he to bewilder us. I still have a letter he wrote me beginning, "Dear parallelepipedon", which sent me scurrying for a definition.

Besides words, a specialty of his was reading aloud books like Pickwick Papers and making them very funny. Then he told exciting continued stories which ran for weeks. They were mostly Western thrillers in which he played the leading role. Thus,

* * * * * * * *

Chapter Nineteen. . . . .

From behind the low hill came a shot. My companion stood ready with gun in hand.

"We're surrounded," he said.

"Look yonder," I exclaimed, "the sheriff's posse are coming along the trail. We must try to hold out till they get here."

Just then another shot rang out and I dropped to the ground.

"They've got me, Mac," I groaned.

Gasps from someone in the audience.

"Did they really shoot you, Mr. Earhart?"

"Did they? I was killed", answered my father seriously. "I lived just long enough to find out whether the posse arrived in time to save the others —but that's the next chapter."

My father's occasional death or his losing an arm or leg was apt to disconcert literal minded neighbor children who happened to be listening.

Sometimes he translated his tales into action and on Saturdays played Indian with any of the neighborhood who wished to join in the games. He was Chief Indian or Chief Scout and the battles which ensued were endlessly exciting. He bore on his nose the marks of one raid, after some *chasee,* during the heat of the battle, had tried to push shut the sliding door to the hayloft just as the Chief Indian had poked his head through the opening.

The barn in Des Moines which was the scene of the Indian Wars and that of my grandmother were the only ones I knew. Being a city child, I was lucky to have any.

Unfortunately I lived at a time when girls were still girls. Though reading was considered proper, many of my outdoor exercises were not. I was fond of basketball, bicycling, tennis, and I tried any and all strenuous games. With no instruction in any sport, I wasn't good enough in myself to excel later. I wish that the vogue of teaching youngsters to learn correct form in athletics had been as universal then as it is now. With the intense pleasure exercise gave me, I might have attained more skill and more grace than I did. As it was, I just played exultingly, and built up all kinds of wrong habits.

For instance, my horse experience is typical. My sister and I spirited lumps of sugar and confections to a neighbor's animal. He was too sleek and too tall for us to manage to get on his back. However, the desire to do so obsessed me to such a point that when a fat delivery animal stopped in front of the house one day I couldn't resist the temptation to get on his back. The curb and the shafts of the wagon harness enabled me to mount. Though I had to be lifted down, I lived for the next experience of the kind. It came through my making the acquaintance of two girls whose father had a butcher shop. Occasionally, when deliveries were not pressing, the girls were allowed to ride the horses who pulled the wagons. They were slightly antique and not exactly the type one would choose in saddle horses. However, there was one heavy-footed sorrel who had evidently had a youth for he bucked with delightful determination for no reason at all. This horse opened vistas of pleasure for me.

Why grandmother didn't wish me to ride I don't know, as my mother had been a beautiful and enthusiastic horsewoman. Perhaps the anxiety and grey hairs she had caused spoiled my chances. Anyway, all my arguments about good stalls going to waste in the barn (except the one occupied by a fierce black and white cow) got me nowhere. Instead, for animals I had to be content, officially at least, with the two cast-iron dogs which sat in the front yard and were patient.

Like many middle western families, we trundled off to a lake (and ours happened to be in Minnesota) for the summer. There another horse entered my life. He was an Indian pony of probably twelve years, but still spry. He could be bribed by cookies to do almost anything. No saddle was available, so half the time my sister's and my riding consisted of walking home. She bears the scars yet of being scraped off his back by an apple tree. It was not until many years later that I had proper riding instruction and I consider that system the reverse of what it should be.

There has been much more attention paid to boys' athletics than to girls'. So much, in fact, that many boys have easy access to coaching in various games as well as track subjects, and most girls do not. Consequently, often little incentive is provided for girls to try to develop athletically and, also, little opportunity, when they do wish to. Usually it is not until girls reach college that any comparative attention is paid to them.

Of course there is more than the mere lack of facilities and teaching to consider. Feminine clothing consisting of skirts, and high heels (after one begins to grow up) certainly make more difficult natural freedom of movement. Then, dresses are much more fragile than masculine garments, so the wearers are usually hampered by being on guard against tearing them.

Tradition hampers just as much as clothing. From the period when girls were not supposed to be able to do anything comes a natural doubt whenever they attempt new or different activities. Whether or not they are fitted to do what men do physically remains to be seen. Tennis, riding, golf and other sports seem not to be harming individuals who are fit, despite dire predictions to the contrary.

I know that I worried my grandmother considerably by running home from school and jumping over the fence which surrounded her house.

"You don't realize", she said to me one day, "that when I was a small girl I did nothing more strenuous than roll my hoop in the public square."

I felt extremely unladylike, and went around by the gate for several days in succession. Probably if I'd been a boy, such a short cut would have been entirely natural. I am not suggesting that girls jump out of their cribs and begin training, but only that the pleasure from exercise might be enhanced if they knew how to do correctly all the things they can now do without injuring themselves or giving a shock to their elders.

Of course, I admit some elders have to be shocked for everybody's good now and then. Doing so, sometimes is a little hard on the shockers, however. I know this for my sister and I had the first gymnasium suits in town. We wore them Saturdays to play in, and though we felt terribly "free and athletic", we also felt somewhat as outcasts among the little girls who fluttered about us in their skirts. No one who wasn't style conscious twenty-five years ago can realize how doubtfully daring we were.

Along with bloomers, coasting while lying flat on the sled was considered rough for girls. Such absurdities, when I looked back on them, make me seem incredibly old. However, that condemned tomboy method of sledding once saved my life.

I was zipping down one of the really steep hills in town when a junk man's cart, pulled by a horse with enormous blinders, came out from a side road. The hill was so icy that I couldn't turn and the junk man didn't hear the squeals of warning. In a second my sled had slipped between the front and back legs of the horse and got clear, before either he or I knew what had happened. Had I been sitting up, either my head or the horse's ribs would have suffered in contact—probably the horse's ribs.

A Christmas letter to my father about this time began somewhat as follows:

"Dear Dad:

Muriel and I would like footballs this year, please. We need them specially, as we have plenty of baseballs, bats, etc. . . ."

Christmas came, and so did the footballs. Sister also triumphantly produced a little .22 popgun, which she had wheedled on her own. But what chances we had to use our new playthings were often spoiled by the realization our activities were frowned upon by those whom we cared for most among grown ups.

As for the gun, after a few short days of popping bottles off the back fence, it mysteriously disappeared. When it was hauled out of a secret hiding place some time later, the explanation that little girls should not go around shooting was given as sufficient reason for its seizure.

As soon as my sister regained possession, she used it for shooting rats in a particularly well inhabited barn. So far, that is the biggest game either of us has ever hunted.

I did trap some though, come to think of it—at the age of six. The trap used was my own invention, too. It consisted of an empty orange crate with a hinged lid. This lay on its side with the lid sticking out like an awning and propped open with a stick. To the stick was tied a long string with me on the other end, hiding behind a tree. When I pulled the string the stick flew out and the lid slammed shut and stayed shut against considerable pressure because of the heavy rubber bands laboriously attached.

What was my game? Nothing more or less than a chicken called by my sister and me in our private terminology a "domineecrips".

Some neighbor's hens occasionally escaped and invaded a special flower bed of ours. Parental remonstrance did no good, so I thought I could solve the problem by catching the invaders one by one. By sprinkling some breadcrumbs around and inside the box, one specimen was lured near enough to be trapped. What a squawking and how the feathers flew, as the surprised bird churned about inside! I was terrified and elated and know how a big game hunter feels after he has captured a charging elephant.

I raced to the house.

"Mother, mother", I panted, "I've caught one of *those* chickens.   What shall we do with it?"

"Why", said my mother, after hearing my brave tale, "give it back, of course.   I'm sure you understand that to keep it would be stealing."

What a blow!   The adventure ended dismally there, except for a glowing memory.

Throughout the grade school period, which was mostly spent in Atchison, I remember having a very good time.   There were regular games and school and mud-ball fights, picnics, and exploring raids up and down the bluffs of the Missouri River.   The few sandstone caves in that part of the country added so much to our fervor that exploring became a rage.

A small band of adventurers worried how to keep exclusive some especially desirable caves.

"Let's put up a sign to scare people", suggested someone.

" 'BEWARE'—that sounds dangerous", said another.

"How do you spell it?"

"B-e-w-e-a-r".

"I think it's B-e-w-a-r-e".

"But bear is spelled b-e-a-r".

"Well, let's put it one way on some and the other way on the others", suggested the arbiter in the crowd.

How terrifying those signs must have been!

The river itself was always exciting.   There usually were large and dangerous looking whirlpools to be seen in its yellow depths, and the banks were forever washing away. Not that any of us ever got very near the banks but—a few of us remembered dimly the floods of 1903 when the water crept up to the gutters of buildings and swept away bridges and spread out over the lowlands as far as eye could see.

One of the particularly entrancing made-up games was called Bogie. It was played in my grandmother's barn and consisted of taking imaginary journeys in an old abandoned carriage. Fortunately next door lived two understanding cousins who were always bursting with ideas. Together we traveled far and wide through hair-raising adventures without ever leaving the barn.

* * * * * * * *

The horses jogged along after an all-day trip.

"Isn't it about time we were getting into the next town?" a passenger remarks nonchalantly.

"If we're on the right road," the driver replies darkly, "we ought to make it by nightfall."

(Studied observations of local geography by all concerned.)

"Let's see a map. This place doesn't look familiar to me," helpfully suggests back seat left.

"I don't remember these swamps at all. And not a house in sight," front seat right chimes in. "Anything might happen."

"WHAT'S THAT OVER THERE?"

* * * * * * * *

Heavens, what was it? I know I can never be so terrified by anything met with in the real world as by the shadowy play creatures which lurked in the dark corners of the hay mow to attack us, or crept up the creaking steps from the lower stalls.

Another favorite Saturday occupation was cooking our noonday meal on a brick oven of our own construction. Fried eggs were the principal dish, as I remember, and we gladly accepted contributions out of the back doors of our respective kitchens to build up the menu. Though I did not care for cooking in school, I liked this particular kind and I believe it started me on certain researches made when I was somewhat older.

These were in the nature of trying to find new foods. I distressed several cooks by boiling up pea pods and corn husks and various other concoctions with which I had hoped to create original and palatable dishes.

I have since found that many of my selections were not unusual at all, and that far more of nature's supplies than I then wot of are used by one people or another as everyday fare.

However, there is one thing I searched for which I am sure has not been used. I had been brought up as regular church and Sunday School attendant in the Episcopal church. Of course, the story of the Children of Israel being fed manna which dropped from Heaven had impressed me deeply. I thought I knew exactly what manna should taste like, and expended a good deal of energy and flour and sugar in trying to reproduce it.

Needless to say, I never succeeded in manufacturing a passable substitute for the celestial food. That it should be small, white, round muffins, a cross between a popover and angel food cake, I was convinced. Perhaps when I give up aviation, I'll attempt production again, for I know that if I could perfect it, there would be an overwhelming demand.

Despite the fun of school, joyful interruptions were occasionally vouchsafed when my father had to make a long business trip. He was, most of his life, connected with one railroad or another, and used to pack the family off when he made a trip of any consequence. Seemingly our jaunts to California and other places did not materially hinder school progress. I think possibly I gained as much from travel as from curricula. Certainly it is something to have lived during the period when into private cars one could invite one's own friends for journeys and meals. Not that we always traveled in private cars, but they were available sometimes. I never bought a railroad ticket until I was sixteen, and even now it doesn't seem quite right. Perhaps that training has done its share in forcing me into various phases of air transportation.

The family rolled around a good deal during my

father's railroad years, Kansas City, Des Moines, St. Paul, Chicago—forward and back. What we missed in continuous contacts over a long period, we gained by becoming adapted to new surroundings quickly. I have never lived more than four years in any one place and always have to ask "Which one?", when a stranger greets me by saying, "I'm from your home town".

I went to at least six high schools but managed to graduate in the usual four years' time. The last one was Hyde Park in Chicago, and it furnished a diploma.

I don't think that boys particularly cared for me, but I can't remember being very sad about the situation. Probably I didn't get so much exercise at dancing as I should have liked, because of having only one or two faithful partners. By the way, I think dancing can be one of the loveliest pastimes in the world. I have always liked it, and among the possessions I treasure most are three volumes of music collected by my grandmother when she was a girl. In them are the popular dance tunes of her day as well as the sentimental songs.

AVIATION AND I GET TOGETHER

AFTER graduation from High School (where I had become greatly interested in chemistry and physics) I waited around a year and then entered Ogontz School, near Philadelphia. During Christmas vacation of my senior year I went to Toronto where my sister was entered at St. Margaret's College. There for the first time I realized what the World War meant. Instead of new uniforms and brass bands, I saw only the results of a four years' desperate struggle; men without arms and legs, men who were paralyzed and men who were blind.

One day I saw four one-legged men at once, walking as best they could down the street together.

"Mother, I'd like to stay here and help in the hospitals", I said when I returned home. "I can't bear the thought of going back to school and being so useless."

"That means giving up graduating," said Mother.

I didn't care. I gave up all thought of returning to school and took steps to become a nurse's aide. Though I endeavored to connect with the American Red Cross, somehow the papers were never completed and I spent months in Toronto working in a hospital until the Armistice.

Nurse's aides did everything from scrubbing floors to playing tennis with convalescing patients.

The patients called us "sister" and we hotfooted here and there to attend their wants.

"Please rub my back, sister. I'm so tired lying in bed." Or, "Won't you bring me ice cream today instead of rice pudding?"

We were on duty from seven in the morning until seven at night with two hours off in the afternoon. I spent a great deal of time in the diet kitchen and later in the dispensary, because I knew a little chemistry. Probably the fact that I could be trusted not to drink up the medical supply of whisky counted more than the chemistry.

When the influenza epidemic struck town, I was one of the few volunteers permitted to be on night duty. I was transferred to a pneumonia ward and helped to ladle out medicine from buckets in the overcrowded wards of the institution.

I believe it was during the winter of 1918 that I became interested in airplanes. Though I had seen one or two at county fairs before, I now saw many of them, as the officers were trained at the various fields around the city. Of course, no civilian had opportunity of going up. But I hung around in spare time and absorbed all I could. I remember the sting of the snow on my face as it was blown back from the propellers when the training planes took off on skis.

Time rolled on and I was still in Toronto at the time of the Armistice. What a day!

All day long whistles kept up a continuous blowing. No means of transportation was available and everyone had to walk downtown, and did so I think. Private cars ran the risk of being stalled in the littered streets and the traction company just gave up and let its trolleys stand. Young men ran around with huge dusters of flour and blew it on young women.

"Hey, girlie, the war's over!" Plop! And the victim looked like a snow man. Supposedly dignified citizens snake-danced and knocked each other's hats off. I didn't hear a serious word of thanksgiving in all the hullaballoo!

At the end of my brief hospital career, I became a patient myself. It was probably the case of trying to carry on all day as usual and work all night. Anyway, I collected a bug which took up residence in the inaccessible little hole behind one's cheek called the antrum. The result was several minor operations and a rather long period of convalescence. Some of this was spent at Northampton where my sister was at Smith and the rest at Lake George. While in "Hamp", I took a course in automobile engine repair, which laid the foundation of any practical knowledge of motors I have gained since.

But I had acquired a yen for medicine, and I planned to fit myself for such a career. Consequently I went to New York and entered Columbia University. There I took what I could of all the "ologies" which should help toward that calling, mixed with a luxury course in French literature. As usual I had a good time, though I studied hard and didn't have any too much money. But stu-

dents in New York can get so much with so little if
they really wish. The steps in the gallery of Car-
negie Hall are really not uncomfortable and I
enjoyed many a concert from that locality—after
I got used to the smell of garlic. Even the Pali-
sades across the river were good for hiking and the
cost to get there by ferry is only a few cents.

I suppose I must have been fairly stalwart-look-
ing for on one of the periodic jaunts to the Pali-
sades, the shopkeeper in a little store where three
other hikers and I had stopped to buy sandwiches
for lunch, eyed our small group and said,

"I bet you girls iss yust off the farm."

It just happened that none of us had ever been
on a farm at that time, but the man behind the
counter was probably not used to city people's
spending their holidays as we were doing.

I was familiar with all the forbidden under-
ground passageways which connected the different
buildings of the University. I think I explored
every nook and cranny possible. I have sat in the
lap of the gilded statue which decorates the library
steps, and I was probably the most frequent visitor
on the top of the library dome. I mean the top.

I used my knowledge of how to get on the dome
a few years later when I was again at Columbia.
It proved an excellent vantage point for watching
the eclipse of the sun in 1925. I stood there with
a well known biologist and looked across at the
angel trumpeting on the highest point of St. John's

Where Amelia Earhart first worked with engines—class in automobile repair at Northampton, Mass. (A. E. is third from the right.)

Cockpit and instrument board
of a fully equipped mail plane

Cathedral. We three appeared to have a better view of the galloping moon shadows than anyone else in the world.

The only other eclipse of the sun I have seen was from the air. I was caught between the mainland and Catalina in the weird darkness of the phenomenon in 1924.

My knowledge of the passageways at Columbia has not yet proved useful, but that could be said of other things one learns at college, too.

It took me only a few months to discover that I probably should not make the ideal physician. Though I liked learning all about medicine, particularly the experimental side, visions of its practical application floored me. For instance, I thought among other possibilities of sitting at the bedside of a hypochondriac and handing out innocuous sugar pellets to a patient with an imaginary illness.

"If you'll take these pills", I heard myself saying in a professional tone, "the pain in your knee will be much less, if not entirely eliminated."

This picture made me feel inadequate and insincere. I did not see then that there was just as much of a problem in curing the somewhat mentally ill as those physically so—even though the methods used might differ.

But when you are young, you are apt to make important decisions for reasons that later on seem quite superficial. And I decided against medicine

in just this way, hearkening to the pleadings of my
mother and father, leaving Columbia and going to
California.

When I left New York I intended to follow up
Medical Research—that, at least, still greatly appealed to me in the field of medicine. But somehow, I did not get into the swing of the western
universities before aviation caught me. The interest aroused in me in Toronto led me to all the air
circuses in the vicinity. And, by dragging my
father around and prompting him to make inquiries, I became more and more interested.

One day he and I were among the spectators at
a meet at Long Beach.

"Dad, please ask that officer how long it takes to
fly", I said, pointing out a doggy young man in
uniform.

"Apparently it differs with different people",
my good parent reported after some investigation,
"though the average seems to be from five to ten
hours."

"Please find out how much lessons cost", I continued.

"The answer to that is a thousand dollars. But
why do you want to know?"

I wasn't really sure. Anyway, such were the
second-hand conversations I had with the patient
pilots of those days. And, somehow or other, I felt
in my bones that a hop would come soon.

The field where I first went up is a residential
suburb of Los Angeles. Then it was simply an

open space on Wilshire Boulevard, surrounded by oil wells. The pilot of the airplane has since become famous as one of the greatest exponents of speed in the world. His name is Frank Hawks and he holds more records for fast flying than anyone else.

As soon as we left the ground, I knew I myself had to fly. Miles away I saw the ocean and the Hollywood hills seemed to peep over the edge of the cockpit, as if they were already friends.

"I think I'd like to learn to fly", I told the family casually that evening, knowing full well I'd die if I didn't.

"Not a bad idea", said my father just as casually. "When do you start?" It would need some investigation I told him, but I'd let him know shortly. Mother seemed equally non-combative.

There were no regular schools at the time, and instruction was mostly given by men who had returned from the war. Within a few days I had signed up for lessons, and went home with the proposition that somebody pay for them.

"You really weren't serious, were you?", my father said in surprise. "I thought you were just wishing. I can't afford to let you have instruction."

I saw if he had ever liked the idea, he was completely unsold then. Evidently, he thought that if he didn't pay, I would not fly. But I was determined, and got my first job—in the telephone company, it was—to pay for the lessons I so dearly wanted.

From then on the family scarcely saw me for I worked all the week and spent what I had of Saturday and Sunday at the airport a few miles from town. The trip there took more than an hour to the end of the carline, and then a walk of several miles along the dusty highway. In those days it was really necessary for a woman to wear breeks and a leather coat. The fields were dusty and the planes hard to climb into. Flyers dressed the part in semi-military outfits and in order to be as inconspicuous as possible, I fell into the same style.

One day as I was striding along the dusty road, a friendly motorist offered me a lift. My costume and destination explained my errand. There was a little girl in the car who became exceedingly excited when she found out for a certainty that I flew.

"But you don't look like an aviatrix. You have long hair".

Up to that time I had been snipping inches off my hair secretly, but I had not bobbed it lest people think me eccentric. For in 1920 it was very odd indeed for a woman to fly, and I had tried to remain as normal as possible in looks, in order to offset the usual criticism of my behavior.

My learning to fly was rather a long-drawn-out process, principally because—no pay, no fly and no work, no pay. However, when the time at last came to solo, the period of training seemed to act to banish nervousness. I went up five thousand feet and played around a little and came back.

"How did it feel?", the watchers on the ground

wanted to know when I returned. "Were you scared?"

"I sang", confessed one pilot who was standing nearby, "as loud as I could."

I felt silly. I hadn't done anything special. My first solo had come and gone without anything to mark it but an exceptionally poor landing.

"You didn't do anything right but land rottenly", said another pilot. "Don't you know you're supposed to be so ground shy you stay up until the gas tank runs dry?"

After I had really flown alone, Mother was good sport enough to help me buy a small second hand plane. It happened to be the only one the builder had so he and I worked out a scheme to use it jointly. For free hangar space to me, he was privileged to demonstrate with it. As both of us were equally fond of the little contraption and equally impecunious, this arrangement worked very well. And I spent many hours in this and other planes I occasionally had a chance to fly.

If Mother was worried during this period, she did not show it. Possibly, except for backing me financially, she could have done nothing more helpful. I didn't realize it at the time, but the cooperation of one's family and close friends is one of the greatest safety factors a fledgling flyer can have.

After a year had passed, I achieved the only type of license issued at that time, the *Federation Aeronautique Internationale*. And Mother was so interested by this time I am sure she would have

accepted a ride with me. However, I didn't start
her aeronautical education until a long while afterward.

In passing I should call attention to the fact that
it wasn't really necessary to have any license at this
period. There were no regulations such as exist
today. People just flew, when and if they could,
in anything which would get off the ground.
Methods of teaching flying have greatly improved
over those of the dim dark ages when I learned.
There were no schools then, as we know them now,
nor standardized equipments. Fundamentally, of
course, the principles are just the same and so are
the fledgling flyers.

Perhaps the easiest way for me to give a picture
of what flying instruction is like is to tell just what
I had to do at first, and to compare that with the
present requirements for obtaining a flyer's license.
As I have said, my training took place in California. The plane used was a Curtiss Canuck very
like the famous Jenny of war time memory. Both
of these planes and their motors, as well, have been
replaced by improved equipment.

In 1920, two years after the Armistice, airplanes
were not so well built as at present and motors had
bad habits of stopping at inopportune moments.
Pilots just naturally expected to have to sit down
once every so often because of engine failure. The
power plants of today are a happy contrast. It is
rare indeed that one "conks", if properly cared for,
so great has been the increase in reliability. Conse-

quently, the modern pilot's attitude is quite different from that of the post war flier.

The development of flying is somehow synonymous with automobiling of a decade ago. If you don't remember, your parents will, the Sunday rides of yesterday. Roadsides were always lined with cars in trouble—some with flat tires, and some with puzzled begoggled drivers peering anxiously under raised hoods at engines they didn't understand. To add to the complications, there were few service stations and few good roads.

Now yours may be among the 20,000 cars going to a football game, say, not one of which will experience a single mechanical failure on the way.

WHEN YOU LEARN TO FLY

EXCLUSIVE of those for glider pilots, there are four types [1] of flying licenses to aspire to at present in the United States. The first is the private license which requires ten hours of solo time—that is, flying a plane alone. The second is the Industrial and the third the Limited Commercial (commonly called the L. C.), both of which require fifty hours solo. The fourth and highest type is the Transport license which requires 200 hours. This last is the only one which unrestrictedly permits its holder to fly passengers for hire or to give instruction.

The cost of obtaining a license varies from an approximate minimum of $300 to a possible out-of-pocket cost of $4,000 for the Transport grade. Of course, all that the schools can give is the training and supervised solo flying. The individual then must be examined by a Department of Commerce inspector, both in written work and in actual flying. The questions are on the plane, the motor, navigation, meteorology, Air Traffic rules and Department of Commerce regulations. The flying consists of landings and take-offs, with air manœuvers which easily show the pilot's proficiency.

In a way, the time and money invested in securing a Transport license is comparable to that neces-

[1] There is also one for autogiro pilots and one called Airline Pilot's License for highly experienced Transport holders; these are rare.

sary for preparing for other professions. A law or
medical student spends several years in college and
emerges the holder of a diploma. The diploma is
really only a permit to gain experience, for the
young lawyer or physician must sometimes work
for a long period before being considered thoroughly competent.

I had just passed voting age when I turned up
for flying instruction. Most of my first lesson consisted in explanations on the ground. I was shown
the two cockpits in the plane and I learned that
the instructor sat in the after-one and the student
in front. I saw the rudder bar and stick and was
told that during instruction these controls are connected so that every movement made by the instructor is duplicated in the student's cockpit and vice
versa. Obviously, therefore, the experienced pilot
is master of the situation at all times, and can correct any mistakes made by the pupil, or show how
manoeuvers should be executed. Much the same
system could be illustrated by imagining automobile driving being taught by utilizing two steering
wheels, duplicate brakes, throttle, and so on.

Piloting differs from driving a car in that there
is an added necessity for lateral control. An automobile runs up and down hill, and turns left or
right. A plane climbs or dives, or turns, and in addition tips from one side to another. There is no
worry in a car about whether the two left wheels
are on the road or not; but a pilot must normally
keep his wings level. Of course, doing so becomes

as automatic as driving straight, but is nevertheless dependent upon senses ever alert.

One of the first things a student learns in flying is that he turns by pushing a rudder bar *the way he wants to go.* (The little wagons most children have turn opposite the push.) When he turns, he must bank or tip the wings at the same time. Why? Because, if he doesn't, the plane will skid in exactly the same way a car does when it whirls too fast around a level corner.

Perhaps you have noticed that the inside of an automobile race track is like a bowl with the sides growing steeper and steeper at the top. The cars climb toward the outer edge in proportion to their speed, and it is quite impossible to force a slow car up the steep side of the bowl. The faster the car goes, the steeper the bank must be and the sharper the turn.

A pilot must make his own "bowl" and learn to tip his plane to the right degree relative to the sharpness of his turn and his speed. A bad skid means lack of control, for a while, either on the ground or in the air, and of course is to be avoided. By the way, compensating for skidding is the same with a car or plane—one turns either craft in the direction of the skid.

The stick—as its name implies—extends up from the floor of the cockpit. It is a lever by means of which the pilot can push the nose of the plane up or down. It also tips the wings. By pushing it to the left, the left wing is depressed, and vice versa.

The rudder bar, upon which one's feet rest, simply turns the nose of the ship left or right, a movement to be coordinated with the action of the stick. Today, by the way, especially in larger planes, a wheel much like the steering wheel of a car is used instead of the simple stick.

In addition to the stick and the rudder, the novice must become familiar with certain instruments placed before his eyes, much as does a driver with a speedometer, gas gauge, etc., installed on the dashboard of his automobile. These instruments include a compass for direction, as well as others which show speed through the air, height above ground, revolutions per minute of the motor, and pressure and temperature of the oil. On planes equipped for all weather flying, several more are necessary.

To get back to my own lessons. After learning as much as I could possibly absorb on the ground, I was taken aloft. For what seemed a long time but was actually only about twenty minutes, I watched the movements of the controls as the pilot, in the rear cockpit, made circles around the field. Finally we landed and she, for my primary work was with a woman, talked with me some more.

The next time I went "upstairs," I was permitted to try to make the plane fly level—and that was very, very hard, indeed. I did exactly what a novice in an automobile is apt to do—overcontrol and wobble about the road, no matter how he endeavors to steer straight.

Besides skidding, a plane can stall as a car does on a hill. *Chug-chug-chug—chug*. Can the motor make the top? *Chu-g-g*. It gives a final gasp and "dies." The car starts to roll downwards, but by jamming on brakes and starting the motor, the driver easily recovers control.

If a plane is stalled, the motor doesn't stop nor does the vehicle slide backwards. Instead, it begins to drop nose first and the pilot has to wait until enough speed is attained to make the rudder and ailerons effective. Of course, with airplanes there is little or no control at slow speeds any more than there is with a motor boat when it is barely moving.

At several thousand feet, a simple plane stall should not be hazardous. However, if it occurs so close to the earth that there isn't time to recover control, a hard landing, sometimes resulting in considerable damage, may be the outcome.

But in the air, as with automobiles, many accidents are due to the human equation. The careful driver, either below or aloft, barring the hard luck of mechanical failure, has remarkably little trouble, considering what he has to contend with.

After I was able to keep the plane pretty level, and go toward a designated landmark with a fair degree of accuracy, I was allowed the exciting experiment of trying to make a turn. After turns came landings, most difficult of all and requiring the most practise. In all, I spent with my instructors about the conventional ten hours, but my student period contained stunting before I soloed.

Perhaps I should explain what stunting is.

The Department of Commerce defines it as "any manœuver not necessary for normal flight." This is a very inclusive definition. I am sure at least a hundred others would be necessary to explain it. Let's try another approach. Just which stunts do flying schools teach? The answer to that query sounds more promising.

The fundamental stunts taught to students are slips, stalls and spins—three S's instead of R's. Loops, barrel rolls and variations and combinations of many kinds are included depending on the instruction desired. The Army, Navy and Marines practise intricate and specialized manœuvers, performing many of them in formation.

A knowledge of some stunts is judged necessary to good flying. Unless a pilot has actually recovered from a stall, has actually put his plane into a spin and brought it out, he cannot know accurately what those acts entail. He should be familiar enough with abnormal positions of his craft to recover without having to think how.

I have always regarded stunting as somewhat similar to driving in traffic. That is, it is a skill attained through practise in order to master a vehicle under as varying conditions as are likely to be encountered. One can choose to drive only on deserted country roads and one can fly only on good

days over regular airways, when neither the knowledge of stunting nor traffic driving may be needed.
But, to get from either craft its best performance
and to be prepared for whatever may happen, both
lessons should be learned.

An individual's life on the ground or in the air
may depend on a split second. The slow response
which results from seldom, if ever, having accomplished the combination of acts required in a given
circumstance may be the deciding factor.

Suppose a car suddenly dashes out from a side
street. Shall the driver on the main highway apply
brakes to avoid a collision, try to get past by step-
ping on the throttle or swerve to one side? The
problem can be worked out easily on paper, but only
experience counts when there is no time to think a
process through. The pilot who hasn't stalled a
plane is less likely to be able to judge correctly the
time and space necessary for recovery than one who
has.

Of course, stunting may be an art if perfected
and practised by those who have the talent. It is
popular for exhibitions where crowds like to see
airplanes doing spectacular loops or dives or flying
upside down. It should be understood that this
precision flying is like tight rope walking—it only
looks easy.

What are the uses of average stunts? Well, side
slips sometimes come in handy in landing in a short
field; stalls and spins in knowing what to avoid in
normal flying. A vertical bank is necessary in a

very short turn and loops and barrel rolls and their relatives and friends are mostly for fun.

I had fun trying to do them, anyway. So much so, in fact, I have sometimes thought that transport companies would do well to have a "recreation airplane" for their pilots who don't have any chance to play in the big transports or while on duty. If a little stunt ship were available, the men could go up 5000 feet and "turn it inside out" to relieve the monotony of hours of straight flying.

The purpose of military stunting is quite distinct from that of civilian brands.

When I learned to fly, a physical examination was not necessary. Today, under the administration of the Department of Commerce, no one may even attempt to learn without first establishing his physical ability.

So the first step taken by the flying candidate must be to secure a medical examination. Throughout the country are physicians designated by the Department as examiners and they make the simple tests. I emphasize simple for myths of having to be whirled in chairs and undergo long trials in complicated machines are still talked about as if they were true.

Primarily the modern examination concerns eyesight and muscular control, but general physical fitness is also a prerequisite. In addition to the familiar test for color blindness and general vision, the determination of depth perception is vital. This means the visual ability to judge distance. In a plane the pilot must know how far he is above the ground (even to a matter of inches, for expert handling) as the wheels skim over the surface of the field before they touch. Just so must a good automobile driver be able to appraise the "holes" in traffic through which he must guide his car without bumping the other fellow.

The depth perception test is made with the applicant sitting about twenty feet in front of a box-like object. Through a small window he sees two upright sticks like miniature goalposts. To one is attached a string which pulls it forward or back. The examiner separates the "goalposts," and the applicant must adjust them so that they seem to be on a line with each other and equidistant from him. Inability to bring them together within the limit of a few millimeters often ends a flying career before it has begun.

A candidate who ultimately seeks only a private license can "get by" with physical imperfections that would make him ineligible for a higher grade. The necessity for wearing glasses, for instance, would disqualify him except in the private classification, and he would be passed for that only if the correction in his lenses was not too great.

Once a license is granted, a pilot is subjected to periodic examinations to keep his rating. This requirement is for checking on physical condition, as well as recording how much flying is being done. If some such practise were followed with automo-

C L I M B

To ascend at a normal angle in an airplane. The angle is seldom steeper than the average hill you climb in your car.

CLIMBING TURN

To ascend at an angle and turn to the right or to the left while climbing. It's like climbing a snake hill in an automobile.

Z O O M

To climb at an angle greater than that which can be maintained in flight. Sometimes a zoom may be almost vertical.

4 5° B A N K

To turn in a circle with the wings at an angle of 45° to the ground. It's like a turn on a high banked automobile race track.

S T A L L

To climb at an angle so steep that an airplane loses its forward speed and "stalls." It does not mean that the motor stops.

VERTICAL BANK

To turn sharply in a circle with the wings in a vertical position. Plenty of altitude is needed when performing this manoeuver.

G L I D E

To descend at a normal or gentle angle without the use of the engine. It's like coasting down hill in an automobile.

D I V E

To descend steeply and rapidly in an airplane, with or without engine power. A dive is the direct opposite to a zoom.

Flying Maneuvers

S P I R A L

To descend in circles not unlike the coils of a spring. It is the opposite to a climbing turn and is a very simple manoeuver.

T A I L   S P I N

A condition resulting from loss of air speed. The airplane spins toward the earth, nose down—not tail down, as some think.

S I D E   S L I P

To descend in a banked position. The plane slips sideward faster than it travels forward. Side slips are often used in landing.

SPLIT ''S'' TURN

Starting as a loop, the airplane makes a 180 degree turn in a vertical bank, coming out in opposite direction.

FORWARD SLIP

To descend in a slightly banked position. In this manoeuver sideward slip and forward travel are approximately equal.

B A R R E L   R O L L

To make a revolution about the fore and aft axis of an airplane. This is a stunt frequently performed by military airplanes.

LOOP INSIDE

To describe a vertical circle in an airplane, nose up and over. This is a military manoeuver and is considered a stunt.

LOOP OUTSIDE

To describe a vertical circle, nose down and under. Only a few aviators have accomplished this. It is the most difficult of all stunts.

Flying Maneuvers

bile drivers, there would doubtless be fewer accidents.

To fly doesn't require a specialized kind of physical make-up. Just normal coordination and good health, necessary to any physical activity, are sufficient. However, to excel in flying, the individual must have exceptional ability, just as a player, to excel in tennis, golf or baseball, must be above the average in his reactions, mentally and physically. Helen Wills Moody, Bobby Jones and Babe Ruth show just as unusual qualifications in their lines, as do Frank Hawks and Colonel Lindbergh in aviation. What I am trying to say is that it doesn't take any more prowess to be a superflyer than it does to be a super something else.

For the normal person there is no particular strain in flying, whether as pilot or passenger, under good conditions. Certainly for the passenger, who has no responsibility, flying can be, by all odds, the pleasantest form of transportation wherever it is practical.

Most people have quite incorrect ideas about the sensation of flying. Their mental picture of how it feels to go up in a plane is based on the way the plane looks when it takes off and flies, or upon their amusement park experience in a roller coaster. Some of the uninitiated compare flying to the memory of the last time they peered over the edge of a high building. But they are mistaken. The sensation of such moments is almost entirely lacking in a plane. Flying is so matter of fact that probably the passenger taking off for the first time will not know when he has left the ground.

I heard a man say as he left a plane after his first trip, "Well, the most remarkable thing about flying is that it isn't remarkable."

The sensation which accompanies height, for instance, so much feared by the prospective air passenger, is seldom present. There is no tangible connection between the plane and the earth, as there is in the case of a high building. To look at the street from a height of twenty stories gives some an impulse to jump. In the air the passenger hasn't that feeling of absolute height, and he can look with perfect equanimity at the earth below. An explanation is that with the high building there is an actual contact between the body of the observer and the ground, creating a feeling of height. But the plane passenger has no vertical solid connecting him with the ground—and the atmosphere which fills the space between the bottom of the plane and the earth doesn't have the same effect.

Many people seem to think that going up in the air will have some bad effects on their hearts. I know a woman who is determined to die of heart failure, if she makes a flight. She isn't logical, for she rolls lazily through life encased in 100 pounds of extra avoirdupois, which surely puts a greater strain on that organ.

Seriously, of course, a person with a chronically weak heart, who is affected by altitude, should not

invite trouble by flying. But if one can go above
sea level safely, one can fly over the Continental
Divide, for instance, with no more effect than if
one drives or goes by train.

Consciousness of air speed is surprisingly absent
when flying. Thirty miles an hour in an automobile, or fifty in a railroad train, gives one a greater
sensation of speed than moving one hundred miles
an hour in a large plane. On the highway every
pebble passed is a speedometer for one's eye, while
the ties and track whirling backward from an observation car register the train's motion.

In the air, there are no stones or trees or telegraph poles—no milestones for the·eye, to act as
speed indicators. Only a somewhat flattened
countryside below, placidly slipping away or
spreading out. Even when the plane's velocity is
greatly altered, no noticeable change in the whole
situation ensues—eighty miles an hour at several
thousand feet is substantially the same as one hundred and forty, so far as the sensations of sight and
feeling are concerned.

"I would gladly fly if we could stay very close
to the ground," is a statement that I have often
heard in one way or another. As a matter of fact,
a plane 100 feet off the earth is·in an infinitely
more hazardous position than one 3600 feet aloft,
all conditions being equal.

One woman told me that she always shut her
eyes when the plane was coming down for a landing, fearing that if she kept them open, she would

be dizzy. It seems to me a fair statement that for the average landing, the descent of the plane is much less noticeable than the dropping of the modern elevator. It comes down in a gentle glide at an angle often much less than that of a country hill. As a result, unless the passenger is actually watching for a landing, he is aware that he is approaching the ground only when the motors are idled.

Trouble in the air is very rare. It is hitting the ground that causes it. Obviously the higher one happens to be, the more time there is to select a safe landing place in case of difficulty. For a ship doesn't fall like a plummet, even if the engine goes dead. It assumes a natural gliding angle which sometimes is as great as eight to one. That is, a plane 5000 feet in the air can travel in any direction eight times its altitude (40,000 feet) or practically eight miles. Thus it has a potential landing radius of sixteen miles in still air.

Sometimes a cautious pilot elects to come down at once to make a minor engine adjustment. Something is wrong and very properly he is unwilling to risk flying further, even though he may be able to do so. Just so the automobile driver, instead of continuing with, say, poor brakes, would do well to stop at once at a garage and have them adjusted. He will then make better time more safely.

All of which obviously points to the necessity of providing frequent landing places along all airways. Few things, I think, would do more to eliminate accidents in the air. With perfected motors the dread of forced landings will be forgotten, and with more fields, at least in the populous areas, "repair" landings would be an added safeguard.

Eliminating many of the expected sensations of flying doesn't mean that none are to be anticipated or that those left are only pleasant. There are poor days for flying as well as good ones. Just as in yachting, weather plays an important part, and sometimes entirely prevents a trip. Even ocean liners are occasionally held over in port to avoid a storm, or are prevented from making a scheduled landing because of adverse conditions. Trains, despite the hundred years since railroads began, are still stalled by washouts and snow. In due time, planes will doubtless become as reliable as these older forms of transportation and learn to overcome their particular weather hazards as well.

The choppy days at sea have a counterpart in what flyers call "bumpy" air over land. Air is liquid flow and where obstructions occur there will be eddies. For instance, imagine wind blowing directly toward a clump of trees, or coming in sudden contact with a cliff or steep mountain. Water is thrown up when it strikes against a rock and so is a stream of air diverted upward by an object in its way. Encountering such a condition, a plane gets a "wallop"—is tossed up and buffeted as it rolls over the wave.

There are bumps, too, from sources other than

these land shoals. Areas of cool air and warm disturb the flow of aerial rivers through which the plane moves. The "highs" and "lows" familiar to the meteorologists—the areas of high and low barometric pressure—are forever playing tag with each other, the air from one area flowing in upon the other much as water seeks its own level, creating fair weather and foul, and offering interesting problems to the students of aviation, not to mention varied experiences to the flyer himself.

The nautical boys have an advantage over the "avigators." Constant things like the Gulf Stream can be labeled and put on charts and shoals marked. But one can't fasten buoys in the atmosphere. Flyers can only plot topography. Air, like water, gives different effects under different conditions. The pilot must learn that when the wind blows over a hill from one direction the result is not the same as that when it blows from another. Water behaves similarly. The shoals of the air seem a little more elusive, however, because their eddies are invisible. If one could *see* a downward current of air or a rough patch of it, plane travel might be more comfortable, sometimes.

"Bumpiness" means discomfort, or a good time for strong stomachs, in the air just as rough water does in ocean voyaging. There is no reason to suppose, however, if one isn't susceptible to seasickness or car-sickness, that air travel will prove different.

Some of the air sickness experienced is due to

lack of proper ventilation in cabin planes. Many are not adequately ventilated for with the opening of windows, the heat and sometimes fumes from the motors are blown in. Adequate ventilation is one of the amenities which the planes of the future will have to possess.

Nervousness over the first ride is probably the greatest cause of air sickness. After the initial journey many passengers never have another sign of it. Of course, some people seem almost determined to be ill. I have heard them say to airline attendants before they get in,

"Well, I'm going to be a very bad passenger today."

"Why do you think so?" asks the transport employee.

"I know I shall be sick." And by concentrating thus on the idea, some do manage very nicely!

However, despite these folk, fewer than five per cent of regular airline passengers succumb. The proportion is certainly several times as great on ocean going vessels on normal days, and many times greater on rough ones.

An interesting result is being noticed as the speed of commercial passenger airplanes increases. On the fast planes almost no airsickness is encountered. The bumps are felt as hard little jolts instead of a slow rocking motion. And the feeling one has is like that in a canoe which rocks lazily on wavelets compared with a very fast motor boat. In a motor boat the waves feel like little bricks against the bottom, but they don't have time to affect the boat much before it has passed by.

Perhaps the greatest joy of flying is the magnificence of the view. If visibility is good, the passenger seems to see the whole world. Colors stand out and the shades of the earth, unseen from below, form an endless magic carpet. If anyone really wishes to see the seasons' changes, he should fly. Autumn turns its most flaming leaves upward and spring hints its coming first for birds and aviators.

I have spoken of the effect of height in flattening the landscape, always a phenomenon in the eyes of the air novitiate. Even mountains grow humble and a really rough terrain appears comparatively smooth. Trees look like bushes and automobiles like flat-backed bugs. A second plane which may be flying a few hundred feet above the ground, as seen from a greater altitude looks as if it were just skimming the surface. All vertical measurement is foreshortened.

The world seen from the air is laid out in squares. Especially striking is the checker board effect wherever one looks down on what his brother man has done. Country or city, it is the same— only the rectangles are of different sizes. The city plays its game of checkers in smaller spaces than the country, and divides its area more minutely.

I am often asked about temperatures in the air. "Is it dreadfully cold up there?"

My answer is that it is likely to be cooler than on the ground, but that temperatures are relative.

As a rule there is a drop of about two degrees for every thousand feet. Thus on a hot summer day the temperatures about 2000 are somewhat lower than those prevailing on the ground, but often one has to go higher to be comfortable. Everyone knows that unless one encounters a breeze, the temperature on a mountain 5000 feet high seems little more agreeable than that at its base. In a small open plane, as contrasted with the cabin ship, one would have a pleasanter time on a summer day, and conversely more discomfort in cold weather—as in an open car. Of course, at really high altitudes regardless of season the mercury drops far below freezing.

Lieutenant Soucek, who holds the international record for altitude, encountered a temperature of 89° below.

JOY HOPPING AND OTHER THINGS

IN 1922, I certainly didn't think of my flying as a means to anything but having fun.

So I turned to other means of making a livelihood. My father's health had begun to be impaired and I attempted commercial photography after a course in the subject through the University of Southern California.

I tried photographing ordinary objects to get unusual effects, and made a number of studies of such things as the lowly garbage can, for instance, sitting contentedly by its cellar steps, or the garbage can alone on the curb left battered by a cruel collector, or the garbage can, well—I can't name all the moods of which a garbage can is capable.

I carried a small camera with me most of the time. Once a new oil well was kind enough to come in just as I was passing in a car, and I caught its first gush with a small motion picture camera and also the oil deluge which followed.

A man jumped out of another automobile. "Pardon me, lady," he said, "were you taking a picture of that oil well?"

"Yes, I was," I answered.

"Well, I'm a real estate operator and I'd like to buy a copy of that film, if you'd care to sell. You see my property's right over there and I'd like to show my prospects what might happen any day in their own yards. What a selling point!" he added as his eyes grew starry.

He turned up to buy the film after it was developed, and the last I heard it was being shown in tent entertainments for prospective buyers and others.

In addition to photography, I carried on in a variety of different occupations including the unconventional ones of being interested in mining in Nevada, and the hauling of building materials by truck locally.

After a year or so of such activities, I decided to return east with my mother and sister who were not particularly fond of the west coast. I wanted to fly east, but the idea seemed so fearful to my family that I finally consented to drive instead. My sister went by train in time for summer classes at Harvard where she was working for a special degree, and Mother and I started by car.

"Which way are we going?" she inquired, as we left Hollywood one morning.

"I'm going to surprise you," I answered, as I headed north instead of east.

Neither she nor I had ever seen some of our best national parks, so I had determined to do some touring. Sequoia, Yosemite, Crater Lake—we peered at all of them in turn. It was June when we arrived at the last, but the road around the ancient cone was still blocked with snow. So I plowed up the coast again.

"Aren't we going east at all?" said Mother, interestedly.

"Not until we reach Seattle," said I with a growing appetite for national parks.

We sampled Canadian scenery at Banff and Lake Louise. While crossing the prairie at Calgary, I lost a precious part of my belongings. At the end of one day, as twilight came on, Mother and I found ourselves on a deserted road without signs of any sort. Our gas was running low and we had no idea how we had arrived where we were. As I rounded a corner, what turned out to be an Indian reservation spread before us.

"This doesn't look very hopeful," I said, "but perhaps I can find someone to ask about roads."

"I see either a wooden Indian or a real one," observed Mother who had been busy looking about.

He was real.

"Where is the main road?" I asked as a starter.

"Unh, papoose," grunted the solemn figure from the depths of his blanket.

I tried again.

"Papoose," came the answer. This time he raised a brown hand and pointed to one of my cherished possessions in the car—a stuffed monkey. Papoose. He wanted the animal for his little Indian. Our situation seemed desperate enough to merit the sacrifice, so I handed him the toy.

"You made the wrong turn five miles back," he informed us. "Follow this road until—" and he finished the directions in perfectly good English. I felt like demanding my monkey back.

The lure of another park began to draw us to Yellowstone, so we returned to the United States. In this curious region it is easy to see the origin of Indian legends of the Great Spirit. With big geysers spouting here and there and the little muddy ones called "paint pots" plopping away continuously during the twenty-four hours, one ignorant of any scientific facts would certainly impute such phenomena to strange gods. Mother said she was almost afraid to go to sleep lest one should plop into bed with her.

As thrilling to me as the national parks were the long stretches of open country dotted with air mail beacons. I saw these first at Cheyenne for the mail route follows somewhat that of the Lincoln Highway. Omaha is one of the oldest stations in the mail development and every time I pass that way I remember the first trip. It is such things which make the real thrills in aviation. I have never been on the ground in this section since, except to drive in from the airport, but I have followed the air route many times.

I finally reached Boston and had so many tourist stickers on the windshield there was little space left to see through it. When I parked the car, groups gathered to ask me questions about conditions of roads, how I'd come, why I'd come, and any number of other questions. The fact that my roadster was a cheerful canary color may have caused some of the excitement. It had been modest enough in California, but was a little outspoken for Boston, I found.

Within a week I had the last of the troublesome operations on my nose, to relieve the condition resulting from my small share in the War. And after I recovered from this I returned to New York and Columbia. Like a great many other girls at this age I had no special plan for myself. But despite my decision against medicine, I was still interested in sciences.

This time I tried some physics as well as other interesting subjects. There was a quiz in physics every week. When I could not answer questions properly I inserted a little French poetry. After the Friendship Flight I received a note from the instructor of this period asking me if on the trip I met any situation difficult enough to be forced into French verse.

> "Mon âme est une infante en robe de parade,
>   Dont l'exil se refléte, éternel et royal,
>   Aux grands miroirs déserts d'un vieil Escurial,
>   Ainsi qu'une galère oublié en la rade."

This and similar noble lines fill space nicely but unfortunately do not count as answers to direct questions.

During my collegiate experience I never sought a degree. I felt somehow my choice of subjects was as good for me as anyone else's. Possibly by the time I am eighty I may know whether I was right or presumptious! At any rate I already know that everything I have studied that I was interested in has given me something.

I returned to Boston and Harvard for the next summer. My sister was teaching and I wanted to try it also. But, as in the west, I did various things, finally ending at a settlement house, as a novice social worker.

The place where I found myself was Denison House, Boston's second oldest social center. It stood in a little island of residences surrounded by warehouses and other buildings in a lower corner of town. The island had at one time been a rather "nice" section and many of the tenements, homes of well-to-do people. The stone fronts of some of the houses, the high ceilings and curving bannisters inside were mute reminders of a more glorious past.

The people whom I met through Denison House were as interesting as any I have ever known. The neighborhood was mostly Syrian and Chinese with a few Italians and Irish mixed in. I had never been privileged to know much about how people other than Americans lived. Now I discovered manner and modes very different from those with which I was familiar. Under my very nose Oriental ideas and the home-grown variety were trying to get along together. The first time I saw, sitting on a modern gas stove, one of the native clay cooking dishes used for centuries by the Syrians, I felt I was seeing tangible evidence of the blending process.

Changes which words underwent in meaning and pronunciation were very interesting to me. The fruit which boarding houses have justly or unjustly made famous was usually pronounced pru-ins in two syllables, instead of prunes. The word "fresh" covered all degrees of misconduct and could be a slight rebuke or an insult. It was funny to hear of a "fresh baby" instead of a naughty one. The Chinese called it "flesh" but kept the same meaning. I wonder what Americans do to foreign words.

I enjoyed visiting the homes of the neighborhood. Now and then when I stayed to meals, some of the articles which long before I had tried in vain to make palatable appeared in delicious form to laugh at me. The Chinese method of cooking peas in the pods, for instance. Through experiences with different foods I came to the conclusion that one can learn to eat anything. The great explorer Stefansson recently told me he had proved that doing so was possible if a certain method was followed.

"On my expeditions to the North," he said, "the rations had to include whalemeat, as that was one of the few kinds of fresh food available. It is usually not palatable at first. I asked several men to undertake an experiment and live *exclusively* on whale meat to see if they could learn to like it. Every time a similar test has been made the results have been the same. For the first few days,

The *Friendship*

Interior of a modern transport plane.

Courtesy Pan American Airways

the men can eat whale meat three times a day without effort. Then they begin to tire of it and eat less and less. For a period they can't bear the sight of it. Soon their intense hunger forces them to nibble and after this stage their appetite gradually increases. At the end of thirty days they have learned not only to like whalemeat, but they never lose the taste for it."

I think I myself can eat anything but oatmeal. Some day I shall have to try out the Stefansson method of learning to like it!

There was always plenty of work to be done at Denison House for there were classes and game periods of all kinds for boys and girls. Besides these, English writing and reading were taught to those ambitious mothers and fathers who knew only their native tongue and came to learn a new one.

This instruction, by the way, is very different from ordinary classes where pupils know the language. Did you ever stop to think how explanations could be made if you did not know any of the words the teacher was using? Of course, she would have to pantomime what she was saying. In the beginning, that is exactly what is done in these classes. For instance, to teach "door," the instructor has to go to a door and point it out. To interpret "I open the door," she must go through the whole motion with the class repeating the words. And so on through the sign language until pupils learn enough to take up the alphabet.

I became so interested in this kind of teaching that I was trying to write a book on it with a co-worker when the Atlantic flight came along, and prevented our finishing it. Since then the number of such classes in settlements and public schools has decreased partly because of the effect of the laws which restrict immigration.

It would have been much easier at Denison House had there been money enough to do all that waited to be done. So few people understood the real needs, that little money was available. We could not have managed at all without the help of the young men and young women who came as volunteer workers from schools and colleges about Boston. They acted as leaders in Boy and Girl Scout groups; they coached dramatics; they taught sewing and basket making and cooking, and told stories to the youngsters in the evening. I often wished my father could have been on tap for some of these groups for I knew his thrillers would have made a hit.

There were sick children who had to be taken to the hospitals and poor mothers who had to have explained to them that hospitals were not dreadful places where their children were imprisoned and tortured by cruel doctors. It is not so easy to understand the ways of a new country when one knows nothing of the laws or customs. Half the trouble caused by the so-called "furiners" is only because no one has taken the trouble to interpret to them the best these United States stand for. Of course, all the interpretation should not be on one side.

In the midst of all these activities at Denison House, not much time was left for flying. However, I did join a chapter of the National Aeronautic Association there and was ultimately made Vice-President. And I did tuck into the busy Denison House days everything I possibly could that had to do with my favorite hobby. I knew some of the local flyers. I went up whenever I had the opportunity. I was busy, too, with Miss Ruth Nichols of Rye in trying to work out some means of organizing the women in the fold. The National Playground Association asked me to be on the Boston Committee to judge in a model airplane tournament they were sponsoring at the time. And since this combined my two greatest interests, aviation and social work, in an unusual way, I was very glad to serve.

None of this was what you could call important —except to me. It was sheer fun. And it did keep me in touch with flying.

It usually works out that if one follows where an interest leads, the knowledge or contacts somehow or other will be found useful sometime. To the person who has learned to swim well comes the opportunity to rescue a drowning man. If I hadn't cared enough to become a member of the aviation group in Boston, there wouldn't have been a *Friendship* crossing for me.

Instead of the elaborate plans which many of the

newspapers insisted I had been making for many
months, the whole expedition was a matter of
chance. It happened as follows.

The invitation to fly the Atlantic came by telephone.

Each afternoon Denison House swarmed with
children released from school. They were of most
ages up to fourteen, practically all sizes and several
nationalities. I had to see, among other things,
that the right children found their way into the
right classes, and that game leaders and instructors
were on the job and prepared. There were always
minor complications. Occasionally the adult workers were late or couldn't come at all. Sometimes
the children were so full of pep, they could hardly
settle down to any one activity. Plaints from those
who never could decide what they really wanted to
do always had to be heard.

"Miss Earhart, I know my lines. Can't I play
games today instead of rehearsing the play?"

"Miss Earhart, I'd rather paint than play
games. Please can't I change periods just this
once?"

After such temperamental problems were solved
for the time, there were others which kept me more
or less on the run until dinner time.

In the midst of such an afternoon in April,
1928, I was called to the telephone.

"I'm too busy to answer just now," I said.
"Ask whoever is calling to try again later."

"But he says it's important to speak with you,"

replied the young messenger, who had been sent to find me.

Very unwillingly I went to the telephone to hear a pleasant masculine voice say,

"Hello. You don't know me, but my name is Railey—Captain H. H. Railey."

Without much more introduction he asked me if I should be interested in doing something for aviation which might be hazardous. Of course, I asked him more about who he was and why he picked me, and what the hazardous undertaking was. This last he wouldn't tell.

Finally, after he had furnished excellent references, and reasons for calling, I made an appointment to see him at his office that very evening. Curiosity is a great starter.

My meeting that night with Captain Railey, who was subsequently in charge of the business affairs of Admiral Byrd's Antarctic Expedition, was very interesting. He told me that a woman had planned to make a transatlantic flight, but for various personal reasons had abandoned the idea of going herself. She still, however, wanted an American to be the first of her sex to cross the ocean by air.

"I might as well lay the cards on the table," finally said Captain Railey. "Would you fly the Atlantic?"

I thought one minute and said,

"Yes,—if." There were still many "if's" in the situation, Captain Railey told me, so I needn't begin on mine. He had simply been asked by a friend of his in New York to cast about for an eligible woman who would go as substitute on the expedition.

Just what the qualifications of eligibility were I have never found out—but I went to New York as a candidate to be looked over. There I learned that the sponsor of the flight was the Honorable Mrs. Frederick Guest of London, the former Amy Phipps of Pittsburgh. She had quietly purchased a tri-motor Fokker from Admiral Byrd and planned to name it the *Friendship* as a symbol of good-will between her own and her adopted country.

"Was I willing to fly the Atlantic?"

"In the event of disaster would I release those in charge from all responsibility?"

"What was my education—if any?"

"How strong?"

"How willing?"

"What flying experience?"

"What would I do after the flight?"

These were some of the questions rained upon me.

It was made clear that the men in the flight were being paid. Having established that, I was asked if I was prepared to receive no remuneration myself. I said "Yes," feeling that the privilege of being included in the expedition would be sufficient in itself.

Ultimately, Bill Stultz, the pilot, received $20,-000 and Lou Gordon, the mechanic, $5000. My own compensation which I had never really seriously considered was, in addition to the fun of the exploit itself, the opportunities in aviation, writing and the like which the Atlantic crossing opened up for me. Incidentally the fees from my newspaper story of the flight went back into the treasury of the enterprise.

Most matters having been settled satisfactorily, there were certain ones to be decided on from my standpoint. I wished to check the equipment and meet the pilot. And I wished to do some of the flying myself. The idea of going as just "extra weight" did not appeal to me at all. Despite my intentions, however, it turned out that was just what I did, for the weather encountered necessitated instrument flying, a type of specialized flying in which I had not had any experience.

It took us twenty hours and forty minutes to cross from Trepassey Bay to Burryport, Wales. In this time the water was visible for only a little more than two hours. We might as well have been flying over the cornfields of Kansas for all we could see of what was beneath. We were in the fog, over it, or between layers for about eighteen of the twenty hours. But I am getting ahead of the story.

Probably few people realize fully what goes on behind the scenes of any major expedition. Whether by horseback or automobile or boat or air, preparations are apt to be long drawn out and worrisome. On the *Friendship* Flight everything had to be tested from the performance of the plane itself, its carrying capacity, speed and other qualifications, to the accuracy of the instruments on which the pilot depends. Then there were the specially installed radio and the three motors with all their many accessories.

Behind the preparations of the moment lay hundreds of hours of flying which Stultz had done, and on Lou Gordon's part, years of experience with engines. There were three in the actual crew of the *Friendship,* though a host of others were employed in the preparatory details. Stultz, originally suggested by Commander Byrd, had an exceptional record as a pilot, and Gordon was selected by Stultz as a thoroughly first-class mechanic.

All work on the project was shrouded in secrecy. That created difficulties for everyone. For instance, no one knew—not even my family—that I had anything to do with the *Friendship*. And as to the plane itself, outside of our own group there was no knowledge of what was planned for it. Ostensibly the Fokker was still owned by Byrd and was destined for the South Pole expedition. That alibi effectively covered the physical preparations of the ship.

I did not dare show myself around Boston Airport, where the ship was being worked on. Not once was I with the men on their test flights. In fact, I actually saw the *Friendship* only once be-

fore the first attempted take-off. Obviously to
have been detected in the picture would have
brought premature publicity, and swamped all
concerned with thrill writers and curiosity seekers.

For flying the Atlantic four years ago was
deemed somewhat more venturesome and jour-
nalistically more spectacular than it is today. I
wonder, for instance, if you know that the *Friendship* Flight was the eighth crossing and that its
crew brought the passenger total up to that time
to thirty? This figure is exclusive of the lighter
than air expeditions. *Since* June 17, 1928, thirty-
one people have crossed the North Atlantic in
heavier than air craft and about twice that number
have made the journey over the South Atlantic.
Approximately five hundred have made it in
dirigibles.

Today an Atlantic flight is, of course, still hazardous. But its chances of success have increased
over those of a few years ago. Airplanes are
faster; engines more reliable and facilities for
weather reporting greatly improved. Today
within a few hours one can get a weather picture of
conditions over the North Atlantic whereas all we
had were relayed at our expense from ships, twelve
to fifteen hours late.

But I think that our desire for secrecy was dic-
tated primarily by what was almost a superstition.
We did not want to talk about what was to be done
until it became an actuality. And by great good
luck, we were able to keep any word of the flight

from leaking out until the *Friendship* was on its way eastward from Boston Harbor.

For the 900 gallons of gas we planned to take, two large elliptical tanks, in addition to those in the wings, were constructed in the cabin. These occupied the space normally used for passenger chairs in the modern airliner. The weight of all filled would be about 6000 pounds, as gasoline weighs a little more than six pounds to the gallon, and the tanks themselves are heavy, too. With the gas we actually took, the *Friendship* weighed more than five tons.

Originally the Fokker was a land plane with wheels, but pontoons had been built and fitted so that it was transformed into a seaplane, the first tri-motor so equipped. In theory, at least, it could land on reasonably smooth seas safely. Pontoons, by the way, not only are supposed to slow down flying speed in the air as opposed to wheels, but may decidedly increase the difficulties of getting off with a heavy load.

The motors to carry the Fokker were Wright Whirlwinds, 225 horsepower each. The width of the wings of the ship was about 72 feet, which is more than twice as broad as most houses are high. They were painted a lovely gold and narrowed gracefully in shape at the tips. The body of the ship, the fuselage, was orange, which blended beautifully with the gold. It was chosen, however, not for artistic effect, but because chrome-yellow, its technical name, can be seen farther than any other

color. In case we had to come down, a little bright
spot bobbing about on the water would have stood
a better chance of attracting attention than one of
neutral tints.

In what space the tanks left in the cabin, a small
table was set up for navigating instruments. Our
rolled-up flying suits and a five-gallon can of water
constituted the available seats. In the cabin floor
was a hatch which had to be opened for each calculation to show drift or actual velocity over the
ground. For, of course, speed over the ground
may not be the same as air speed.

Airplanes are equipped with air speed indicators
which tell the pilot how fast a stream of air is
passing the wing of the ship. If there is little or no
wind, it may read approximately true for ground
speed. It reads the same whether the plane is flying with the wind or against it. A plane which
travels 100 miles in still air would be going only
eighty miles an hour over the ground if a twenty-
mile wind blew against it, head on. But the air
speed indicator doesn't know the difference and
gives its hundred m.p.h. reading just the same.
Conversely, if the twenty-mile wind were blowing
in the *same* direction as the airplane was flying, the
speed of the plane would be increased to 120 miles
per hour. So there must be other means of determining actual ground speed. Over a mapped territory the pilot without much trouble can clock his
speed with the landmarks he can recognize.
Where landmarks aren't available, different types

of indicators are used to make the calculation.

While preparations for the flight were progressing, I carried on with my job at Denison House.
No one there, except the head worker, knew I was
concerned with flying the Atlantic, for I continued
to supervise as well as I could the varied activities
which fell to my lot.

Toward the end of May we were ready to go—
more or less ready, anyway. In a chartered tug
one dawn, we put out to the *Friendship* at her
moorings off East Boston. But our first attempt
came to naught, as we did not get away.

Twice the experience of trying to start was repeated. Once there was too little wind for the
Friendship to rise from the water, and once too
much fog.

> *The fog comes on little cat feet and sits on
>   its haunches
> Overlooking city and harbor
> And then moves on.

I can quote Mr. Sandburg's charming poem with
enthusiasm as I write this. However, I can't say I
appreciated it the day of the second unsuccessful
take-off when the fog he sings of descended to
dampen us spiritually as well as actually and to
keep us on the ground for the time.

Despite its poetic possibilities, fog, of course, is
one of the great hazards of flying. From the air,
when one cannot see the horizon, there is nothing

* We are indebted to Henry Holt & Company, Publishers, for permission to reprint this extract of "*Fog*" from Sandburg's "*Chicago
Poems.*"

much on which to base knowledge of one's position in space. Only the instruments which have been developed in the last few years can be trusted to tell whether one is upside down or right side up. The poor old senses, which serve us so well so often, don't send the correct impressions to the brain in this instance at all.

Just how far one may be deceived in this way was once clearly shown to me by a certain test. I was blindfolded and put in a chair which could be noiselessly revolved. The examining physician began to turn the chair slowly to the right.

"Which way are you turning?" he asked.

"To the right," I answered smartly.

"Now which," he asked a moment later.

"Left," I answered promptly.

"Lift up the bandage and look."

I did. I wasn't turning at all.

"If you had not made the mistake you did, you would not have been normal," said the doctor cheerfully.

Then he explained that when he first began to turn the chair the direction registered on my brain correctly. If he changed the speed of rotation or stopped, I received the impression I was turning in the opposite direction. Nothing but the sight of objects I recognized or some instrument which could not be fooled could make me believe the direction of the turn was not reversed.

The following is an interesting test which you may experiment for yourself:

If you would like to see what you can do—or can't—when you are unable to see, try to walk blindfolded in a straight line. You had better go where there is plenty of room and have someone walk closely behind you lest you run into something. Pick out a point several hundred feet away, and then see where you are at the end of the time it would have taken you to reach your objective.

In thick or heavy rain or snow, a pilot is just as blind as if he had a black cloth over his eyes. Consequently he will make the same mistakes as I did in the chair, if he does not have unbiased instruments to tell him the truth. Thus the plane might be in a steep spiral and he might be trying to right it by doing unknowingly the very thing which would tend to keep it so. I do not wish my statement to sound as if all any flyer had to do in "soupy" weather is to look at a few instruments, flap his wings and away. It must be remembered that reading and reacting to instruments require practise and skill.

As with music, for instance. One might well say to any random individual, "Here is a sheet of music and there is a piano. Go ahead and play." It would be absurd to expect faultless execution without the subject's understanding and his repeated performance.

To complicate matters, instruments for blind flying are not yet perfected, neither those for the cockpit nor those which are a part of ground equipment.

ACROSS THE ATLANTIC WITH THE
FRIENDSHIP

WHEN the *Friendship* finally got off at Boston, she was headed straight up the coast for Newfoundland. There, at Trepassey, we intended to take on a supply of gasoline which had been stored in advance, why or for whom no one knew.

Owing to local weather it was impossible to go farther than Halifax the first day. More fog. We came down through a hole in it and put in at the harbor. News of our destination had leaked out at Boston soon after our departure, and in the Nova Scotia hotel where we spent the night, I had my first taste of the "inquiring reporter" who inquired so persistently that sleep was impossible.

In our brief stay at Halifax, we suffered a bit from holidayitis. In the first place it was Sunday. Then, as I remember, it was Orchard Day, and the birthday of the King, to boot. Everybody was away celebrating so that getting fuel proved an acute problem. But get it we finally did and as the day was gorgeously clear with a fine following wind, we were able to take off about nine. Indeed weather conditions were so nearly ideal that had it not been necessary to refuel, we should have passed Newfoundland by entirely and continued on our way eastward.

In Trepassey there was plenty of trouble. Weather and mechanical difficulties combined to keep us in the hamlet on the coast of Norman's Woe for thirteen days, instead of two or three as we had counted upon.

I hope some day to return to Trepassey really to enjoy its fishing and hunting and to renew acquaintance with its hospitable people. During our visit we were under too much strain to think of anything except vital matters like weather reports, gasoline consumption, leaking pontoons, oil lines and the like.

Two Trepassey memories which stand out particularly are of the lovely hooked rugs and the excellent trout streams of Newfoundland. The coast is a graveyard of wrecked ships, and from the wrecks, I was told, come most of the materials used in the rugs. Much of the silver encountered in the fishermen's homes has the same origin, as can be seen by the names of lost ships it bears.

Of course, what comes up from the sea out of ships generally belongs to the finder, with no questions asked. If the other fellow's loss is forgotten, I have often thought how exciting it would be to open boxes and barrels brought in by the tide. Like the bottle and pill box in "Alice in Wonderland" with their enticing, "Drink me" and "Eat me," I am sure these floating surprise packages must say almost audibly "Open me! Open me!"

Newfoundland people come principally from England, Ireland and France. Originally, as I understand it, they were supposed to return to their homeland at the end of each fishing season.

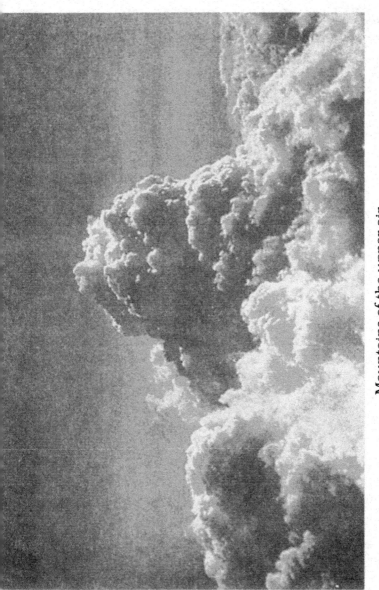

Mountains of the upper air

One of Pan American's Clipper ships

However, some of them strayed and stayed, and from these pioneers largely descended the inhabitants of today.

Quite different from the barrenness of the coast is the hospitality of the people. Little as they had, they shared it gladly with the strangers who had dropped down out of the skies. As a matter of fact, air visitors were no novelty to them. The Italian round-the-world flyer, de Pinedo, had been marooned there for many days in 1929 and the NC Navy flyers of 1919 had started from Trepassey with their giant sea planes.

As it took a week for the mail to come from Boston and as our friends in the "States" had not expected us to linger long in Trepassey, no mail caught up with us. But many messages reached us by telegraph, and eventually a newspaper correspondent from St. John's came in on the little train which charges down from Newfoundland's capital twice a week.

So long did we linger perforce in Trepassey that the natives began to think the *Friendship* couldn't fly. During the first days of our stay, many came over from neighboring villages, and all who hadn't seen our plane land seemed to feel we had taxied in and had never been off the water at all.

Unless the wind blows from a certain direction, Trepassey harbor is too narrow for take-off with a heavy load. When the "blow" is from the southeast, which is best for the take-off so far as the terrain is concerned, it brings in the fog that hangs forever off-shore, where the warm gulf stream meets the colder waters of the north.

Thus we had to take advantage of the moment and be ready to hop off when conditions were right, as they changed rapidly. Ultimately we were obliged to alter our plans for carrying 900 gallons of gasoline, barely contriving to get off with 700. This lessened supply decreased our margin of safety and shortened our cruising range. At best, we hoped only to reach Ireland, and for days we seriously considered the possibility of trying to make the Azores, when our representatives in New York notified us that gas was obtainable there.

One of the questions which has been asked me most frequently is what we ate on the actual flight. We had with us scrambled egg sandwiches, made fresh in Trepassey, coffee for the men (I don't drink coffee unless I have to and a special promised container of cocoa for me somehow didn't materialize), a few oranges, a bottle of malted milk tablets, some sweet chocolate and five gallons of water. Then, in case we were marooned, we had an emergency ration called pemmican, a very concentrated food used by explorers. A spoonful or so a day is supposed to keep one healthy and happy. After testing this concoction, which is reminiscent of cold lard with dark unidentified lumps floating in it, I question the degree of happiness obtainable, whatever the health content.

Actually on the trip there was so much to do and think about that none of us seemed to be hungry.

I ate six malted milk tablets and two oranges, and I think the men consumed about the same quantity, washed down by coffee. Somehow or other under the strain of excitement, no one seemed to feel like eating. And then, after all, twenty hours is not so long to go without sleeping or eating, if one is in good physical condition.

About eleven on the morning of June seventeenth, the wind was reasonably right, and the weather forecast as relayed to us from New York, not too unpromising. So again we taxied to the end of the harbor and faced into position before the wind.

With the waves pounding the pontoons and breaking over the outboard motors, we made the long trip down its length, the ship too heavy to rise. Stultz turned around and taxied back to try again.

I was crowded in the cabin with a stop watch in my hand to check the take-off time, and with my eyes glued on the air speed indicator as it slowly climbed. If it passed fifty miles an hour, chances were the *Friendship* could pull out and fly. Thirty —forty—the *Friendship* was trying again. A long pause, then the pointer went to fifty. Fifty, fifty-five—sixty. We were off at last, staggering under the weight carried with the two sputtering outboard motors which had received a thorough dousing of salt water.

We had made so many false starts, practically no one was on hand to see our real departure. I had left a brief telegram announcing it to be sent half an hour after we were actually in the air. This was my last message to New York.

Our Atlantic crossing was literally a voyage in the clouds. Incidentally the saying about their silver linings is pure fiction. The internals of most clouds are anything but silvery—they are clammy grey wetness as dismally forbidding as any one can imagine. However, some air travelers know that above them there is a different world from any encountered elsewhere. If really on top of a solid cloud layer, the sun shines brightly over a fluffy sea with a brilliance more blinding than that of snow fields. Or as it sinks, the clouds may be colored as beautifully from a bird's-eye view, as when we see them at sunset from the earth. Of course, from an altitude of several thousand feet, the sun can be seen longer before it drops below the horizon. And as evening falls, it is really brighter "upstairs" than on the ground.

I kept a log of the *Friendship* Flight and find I mention clouds more often than anything else.

Log book: "I do believe we are getting out of the fog. Marvellous shapes in white stand out, some trailing shimmering veils. The clouds look like icebergs in the distance. It seemed almost impossible that one couldn't bounce forever on the packed fog we are leaving. The highest peaks of the fog mountains are tinted pink with the setting sun. The hollows are grey and shadowy." Or again: "We are running between the clouds still, but they are coming together. . . . How grey it is before; and behind, the mass of soggy cloud we came through, is pink with dawn. Dawn 'the rosy fingered', as the Odyssey has it.

"Himmel! The sea! We are 3000. Patchy clouds. We have been jazzing from 1000 to 5000 where we now are, to get out of clouds. At present there are sights of blue and sunshine, but everlasting clouds always in the offing."

In the northern latitude in which we flew, the late June days were remarkably long. It was actually light until ten o'clock at night and dawn or its approximation appeared before three in the morning. In the hours between, there was little complete darkness unless we were blanketed with fog. Otherwise as the sun moved around the world, we thought we could see a pale glow marking its course, far to our left.

Log book: "5000 ft. A mountain of cloud. The North Star on our wing tip. My watch says 3:15. I can see dawn to the left."

The highest the *Friendship* climbed was 11,000 feet to get over a bank of clouds which reared their heads like dragons in the morning sun. The lowest we flew was a few hundred feet along the coast of Wales. Some of the clouds over the Atlantic held rain, and every time the plane plowed through them the outboard motor would cough and complain. They did not like being wet because they had been caked with salt water on the take-off and the salt had dried to make a contact for the sparks to jump from the plugs.

If the *Friendship* had come down on the water
and had not floated, we should have been in a sorry
plight for to save weight we had left life-savers behind and also the rubber boat which we originally
planned to take. That little boat I now use in
summer for sport at the beach at Rye. It can be
blown up in a few moments and won't capsize;
while its capacity load has never been determined.

The sun, as I have said, went to bed late and got
up early. The 11,000 feet the plane was forced to,
as morning came, was not high enough to climb
over the clouds piled in front of her like fantastic
gobs of mashed potatoes. Bill Stultz checked his
gasoline and concluded we should waste too much
if he went higher in an effort to surmount them.

By that time we were nearing our last few hours
of fuel. So the nose of the *Friendship* burrowed
down into the white clouds and we descended
quickly through the grey wetness to about 2500
feet.

Log book: "We are going down. Probably Bill
is going through. Fog is lower here too. Haven't
hit it yet, but soon will so far as I can see from the
back window. . . . Everything shut out.

"Instrument flying. Slow descent first. Going
down fast. It takes a lot to make my ears hurt.
5000 now. Awfully wet. Water dripping in window."

The reference to my ears hurting simply records
a rather swift descent. When a plane comes down,
it necessarily enters air which grows more dense

near the earth's surface. The increased pressure on the body is noticed most on the eardrum, particularly if any of the passages are stopped, as when one has a cold. If the change from the higher to the lower altitude is made gradually enough, normally no sensation is present. However, if the drop is very rapid and through a considerable distance, the reaction may range from unpleasant to painful. Indeed, it would be possible to rupture eardrums in a very fast dive continued through many thousand feet. The same condition obtains in going below the surface of water. A diver must accustom himself gradually to the greater pressures as he goes down to prevent pain or permanent injury. He must also be careful about coming up too quickly, for in decreasing pressure adjustment is needed also.

Bill Stultz didn't care whether he made us conscious of our descent or not. He was doing what he thought best, and a little temporary discomfort was of no consequence. Finally the *Friendship* was levelled off and we cruised along where we could now and then see a bit of water through occasional holes beneath us.

Although I have told it before in print, I should repeat the story of our most exciting moment. Our radio equipment had been silent after eight o'clock the first evening. Consequently instead of getting word from ships to help us check our position we had to depend solely upon dead reckoning.

According to our calculations the time had come

for us to see Ireland. However, if we had mistaken
our course and gone out of our way, then with our
diminishing supply of gasoline, our situation might
be serious. Minutes passed and we saw no Emer-
ald Isle.

But suddenly out of the fog, on a patch of sea
beneath us, appeared a big transatlantic vessel.
Instead of its course paralleling ours, as we thought
it ought to, it was going directly across our path.
Its action was unpleasantly puzzling. After all,
were we lost?

We circled around the vessel, hoping that the
Captain would guess what we wanted and have the
bearings painted on the deck for us to read. But
nothing happened. Then I wrote out a request
that he do so, put the note into a bag with a couple
of oranges for ballast, and tried to drop it on the
deck, through the hatchway in the bottom of the
plane. But my amateur bombing did not work;
my aim was faulty and the two oranges landed in
the water some distance from the ship.

What to do? We couldn't expend further fuel
in aimless circling. If our course was really wrong,
should we give up, land in the water beside the
unknown vessel, and be hauled aboard in safety, or
should we stick to our guns and keep going, trust-
ing in the accuracy of our observations?

Tacitly, the crew agreed to follow through. We
knew we had about two hours' gas or a little less
than that left, and it seemed sensible to use it up
in an effort to complete the job.

So we kept on eastward. The diary records the tenseness of the moment. Log book: "Can't use radio at all. Coming down now in rather clear spot. 2500 feet.

"8:50 2 boats!!!! (These were two little ones which not only didn't disturb us but gave us pleasure as the first sign of life we had seen.) Then. Trans steamer. Try to get bearing. Radio won't (I meant wouldn't respond to Stultz's frantic calls). One hr's gas. Mess. All craft cutting our course. Why?"

"Mess" expressed our situation as well as any single word I could think of at the time—our puzzlement, our helplessness with a diminishing fuel supply, our exasperation at our inability to communicate with the ship just below us.

It turned out the ship was the *America,* commanded by Captain Fried. Later he told me that every time he had learned of a contemplated crossing by air he had seen to it that bearings were painted on the deck every two hours in the hope that the flyers might come his way. But none ever had. Of our flight he had heard nothing in advance so his paint pots were not in readiness. For this lack of preparedness he afterwards apologized to me profusely, and, I understand, has since kept cans of paint ever ready to serve in a similar emergency.

As it turned out, we were within a few miles of the mainland when we sighted the *America.* Though we did not know it, Ireland had been passed and we were nearing Wales, facts which accounted for the diagonal course of the *America* proceeding through the Irish sea.

Soon after the fruitless orange bombing, we saw several fishing vessels so small that we knew they could not be many miles off shore. What shore we did not know—or care.

Just as the *America* had loomed out of the fog, so land appeared. In the previous hours we had seen so many dark clouds which looked like land that at first we thought this new shape was simply more shadow geography. But it stayed, undissolved, and grew larger through the mist and rain. Land it was, very definitely.

Very low we skirted the cliffs against which the sea was beating, and looked down on a story-book country-side of neatly kept hedges, compact fields and roadways lined with trees.

The *Friendship* had to follow water, for being fitted with pontoons, we did not dare cross large areas of unfamiliar land, particularly with only a few gallons of fuel in the tanks. After some minutes of cruising along the shore, we came to what seemed a break in the channel we were following, and decided to descend near a little town. That landing, we knew, would be the end of the journey, for it would not be possible to take off again with the quantity of fuel we had left. So low it was by this time that the engines were supplied only when we were flying level.

Stultz set the *Friendship* down in mid-channel

and taxied to a heavy marking buoy, to which the men made the plane fast to keep her from drifting in the swift tide. Then, having crossed the Atlantic by air, we waited for the village to come out and welcome us.

The buoy was about half a mile from shore and probably our craft looked no more exciting than any other seaplane. There were three men whose identities I should like to know working on the railroad along the water's edge. Certainly no philosophers could have cultivated more incurious or placid natures than they. They looked us over, waded down to the shore, and then calmly turned their backs and went to work again.

Perforce we stayed on the *Friendship* and waited for something to happen. Time passed and nothing did. After a while, groups of people slowly gathered in the rain. Slim Gordon crawled out on the pontoons and called for a boat, to no avail. Probably if the townspeople heard it at all, his American sounded as strange to the Welsh people as their own language did to us. Something like this that was—lmnpqrs.

"I'll get a boat," I said finally, and squeezed forward into the cockpit. Out of the open window I waved a white towel as a signal of distress. At my gesture a friendly gentleman on shore took off his coat and waved cordially back at me. But that was all.

Finally boats did begin to come out. Yet, even after the first one returned to shore with news of our arrival, it was several hours before the *Friend-ship* was sailed into her mooring place for the night and her crew were able to disembark.

Though we had been scheduled to arrive at Southampton, the weather was too threatening to fly on, and the three musketeers began to need food and rest, although we did not get either very soon. Actually I think dinner was served about ten, after the rigors of a welcome at the hands of 10,000 enthusiastic Welshmen, disciplined by three flustered policemen.

Since our visit, these kindly people of Burry Port have erected a monument in our memory. It stands eighteen feet high and bears this inscription.

"Erected in commemoration of Miss Amelia Earhart of Boston, U. S. A., the first woman to fly over the Atlantic Ocean. Also of her companions Wilmer Stultz and Louis Gordon. Flew from Trepassey, Newfoundland, to Burry Port in 20 hours and 40 minutes in the seaplane Friend-ship, on June 18, 1928."

The day after our arrival in Wales we flew the *Friendship* from Burry Port to Southampton. On this stretch I did some of the flying—the only time during the trip. The harbor at Southampton was crowded with craft of many kinds, and Bill Stultz had something of a task to find a clear space in which to land. For some time we circled about in doubt, until suddenly the green lights of a signal gun fired from a rapidly moving launch indicated where the reception committee wished us to come down.

Once on the water, the launch drew alongside and took the three of us ashore. That was the last I saw of the *Friendship,* and unfortunately the last any of us saw of the charts and other paraphernalia used on the flights. We might have cherished some articles, had they not disappeared, for our respective grandchildren. The malady of collecting souvenirs seems to be universal in its scope—but one grandchild's loss is another one's gain.

For instance, when we landed at Burry Port my entire baggage consisted of two scarfs, a toothbrush and a comb. One scarf was quickly snatched by some enthusiast, I don't know just when. The other stayed with me because it happened to be tied on. The toothbrush and comb also survived, probably because they were hidden in the community duffle bag, shared by Stultz, Gordon and me.

By the way, the absence of baggage—even a change of clothes—seemed to provoke much interest, especially among women. I had no intention whatever of trying to set a fashion in transatlantic air attire. My traveling wardrobe was due entirely to the necessity of economizing in weight and space. I had landed in exactly what I wore and nothing more, and knowing this, my English friends kindly saw to it that I was generously outfitted. So much publicity was given to my lack of wardrobe that some weeks later when I reached New York with three trunks it was impossible to

protest duties that were levied by cruel customs
men upon my purchases and my gifts!

The *Friendship* was sold to an American and by
him later to three South American flyers who
planned another crossing of the Atlantic. Their
project was not fulfilled, and recently I was told
that the faithful old plane has become the air force
of a band of revolutionists in South America.

At Southampton Mrs. Frederick Guest, sponsor
of the flight, met us. More than ever then did I
realize how essentially this was a feminine expedition, originated and financed by a woman, whose
wish was to emphasize what her sex stood ready
to do.

To me, it was genuinely surprising what a dis-
proportion of attention was given to the woman
member of the *Friendship* crew at the expense of
the men, who were really responsible for the flight.
The credit belongs to them and to the flight's
backer as well as to the manufacturers of the plane
and motors. This thought I have tried to bring
out at every opportunity.

But I happened to be a woman and the first to
make a transatlantic crossing by air, and the press
and the public seemed to be more interested in that
fact than any other. Though palpably unfair, the
circumstance was unavoidable. I think in the future, as women become better able to pull their own
weight in all kinds of expeditions, the fact of their
sex will loom less large when credit is given for
accomplishment.

Some·day I shall go back to England and see all the things I didn't get enough of on my hurried visit. The memory of my two weeks in London is a jumble of teas, theatres, speech making, exhibition tennis, polo and Parliament, with hundreds of faces crowded in.

Nevertheless, a few particular incidents stand out. One is a vivid recollection of the gracious and brilliant Lady Astor. On my visit to her beautiful country place she led me to a corner and said:

"I'm not interested in you a bit because you crossed the Atlantic by air. I want to hear about your settlement work." I was glad to find someone who regarded me as a human being, and after I told her of seeing Toynbee Hall upon which Denison House was patterned, she promised to send me a couple of books she thought I might like to read. She did and I did.

Like Christopher Robin, I enjoyed seeing the changing guard at Buckingham Palace—perhaps because it amused him. Driving to the left-hand side of roadways was as interesting as a new game to me, accustomed to American traffic rules.

"Should you like to meet the Prince of Wales?" This was the first question I was asked in a consolidated interview of newspaper writers.

"That depends on his Highness' wishes," an American official answered for me, courteously and correctly.

I said not a word myself, as his reply was eminently satisfactory. The next day in an English daily was published my supposed reply, to wit:

"Wal, I sure am glad to be here, and gosh, I sure do hope I'll meet the Prince of Wales." I preserve this clipping among my most precious souvenirs.

Perhaps the implied nasal twang of the alleged quotation explains why I never did meet the Prince.

After a fortnight of seeing London and being seen, we headed home again on the steamship *Roosevelt*. How thoroughly we enjoyed the restfulness of this voyage which afforded really the first relaxation since our departure from Boston! We were allowed by Captain Harry Manning to loll at will on the bridge.

"Can't you take us to South America instead of New York?" was an almost daily question from us to him. We tried in vain to have him alter the course of the *Roosevelt* and land in some pleasant country where no one knew us. For all three of us dreaded the inevitable receptions and longed for the ocean to stretch itself indefinitely.

In spite of our dread, homecoming was really an event. The reception at City Hall in New York and the presentation of medals there and in Boston and Chicago followed closely upon our landing. Riding up Main Street while people throw telephone books at you is an amusing modern version of a triumphal march.

Three years ago the returned aviator still rated

A typical Department of Commerce beacon

Checkered countryside as seen from approximately
30,000 feet altitude

spectacular headlines. He was front page "news,"
she was even front-pager (again the accident of
sex).

In all, I think thirty-two cities asked us to visit
them. Speedily I discovered I was a native of Boston, Kansas City, Chicago, Des Moines, Los Angeles and several way points. (I have told you before of my childhood in many states.)   At all
events, though the friendliness and undeserved
honor of their invitations were appreciated, it was
impossible to accept many of them.

On the advice of those who helped me, we first
went to several cities, and then so far as I was
concerned, went into retirement. Had the prof-
fered schedule been accepted I might not have got
home for a year and a day.

But even the retirement was reasonably strenuous. Today, if you ever figure in any unusual exploit, be it a flight, a voyage in a small boat, or,
say, a channel swim, paraphrasing Alice in Wonderland, "There's a publisher close behind you who
is treading on your heels." Writing a book seems
inevitable. My "porpoise" wanted his book in a
hurry. They always do, and so the first weeks of
"rest" were devoted to completing a little volume
called *20 hrs. 40 min.*

Between chapters I talked to editors, promoters,
airline operators, and educators with propositions
generous, preposterous, or inviting. Before any
commitments were made, the book was completed.
Clearly, it was time to get into the air again.

In England, I had purchased a small sport plane from Lady Mary Heath. It was the one she had flown alone from Cape Town to Croyden. Its fuselage was studded with medals and mementoes of her historic flight, and when she turned it over to me, she put on another. It says, "To Amelia Earhart from Mary Heath. Always think with your stick forward." In other words when your attention wanders, be sure the nose of your plane is down to maintain flying speed for safety.

Just as the book was about finished, the Avro arrived, and between correcting last chapters, I flew it from a nearby polo field. Then with the final proofs of the book ready, I purchased a lovely assortment of air navigation maps and headed for California and the National Air Races there.

I still had no plan for myself. Should I return to social work, or find something to do in aviation? I didn't know—nor care. For the moment all I wished to do in the world was to be a vagabond—in the air.

VAGABONDING

THAT initial flight of mine across the continent proved to be a pleasant interlude. I later found that it marked the first solo trip a woman had made from the Atlantic to the Pacific and back again.[1] But at the time it was to me primarily a vacation—a minor adventure in vagabonding by air and a relaxation from writer's cramp.

The first stage of my hobo journey took me to Pittsburgh, Dayton, Terre Haute, St. Louis, Muskogee, and on into New Mexico. After straying from the course, I finally landed at Pecos, Texas.

Automobilists universally complain about the lack of parking space. For vehicles of the air the absence of landing fields may be even more inconvenient. When a plane's motor fails—an occurrence becoming rarer every day—the pilot must make a landing. True, the machine can be controlled from the air and made to glide gently down without the engine running, but it must have a smooth open space for alighting.

As there is always the possibility of some failure in anything man-made, so even with the well behaved motors today, occasional descents are inevitable. And when they come, "parking space" is es-

[1] I can find no records to controvert this statement.

sential. The field need not be elaborate, although
naturally the pilot turns with delight to the large
well-kept airport offering hangar service and complete equipment. But where air travel does not
warrant great expenditures, a smooth parking
space is gratefully used.

As I have said, it is sometimes wise for a pilot to
bring his plane down to make a minor adjustment
which he couldn't do in the air. Or he may elect to
wait till a storm has passed rather than try to fly
through it. Under these circumstances, he may not
be so hard put as he is with his motor entirely out,
nevertheless safety demands a place to land.

And oh, for a country-wide campaign of sign
painting! Coming down through a hole in the
clouds, any flyer is thankful for definite information
as to his location, even if it is only to check his
navigation. If he is off his course, it may be im-
perative to know where he is in order to safeguard
his gasoline supply. Approaching darkness or the
necessity for a repair landing makes minutes extremely precious. At such a time, a name on a
sign may be a real life saver. Too, inexperienced
pilots especially need such added aids to their cross-
country flying.

There is also another side to this sign painting
business. The city in which you live should be
proud enough of itself to be recognized by air
travelers. Often the thousands who pass by on the
airways can't do so unless the name is prominently
displayed. Though there has been much progress

made in the past few years, there is many a community whose shingle might be hung out for the air
traveler.   Large white or chrome yellow letters
painted on some flat roof should announce the
names of all progressive cities and towns to the
flying world.   An arrow pointing the direction to
the nearest landing field is also desirable.

Imagine automobiling without signs! Imagine
trying to recognize a new town, the way flyers do—
a hundred-mile-an-hour look at a checker-board of
streets and roofs, trees and fields, with highways
and railroads radiating and crisscrossing and perhaps a river or two to complicate—or simplify—
the geography lesson.

On my own transcontinental air-gypsying, I saw
few towns properly named.   In some, the airway
sign boards had been so neglected that the lettering
was dirty and almost illegible; in others the only
words visible from above spelled the names of certain kinds of pills or liniment.   The Chambers of
Commerce in many communities may be asleep to
the value of aerial advertising, but the patent medicine vendors are not. They often paint their signs
on sloping roofs to be read alike by those who pass
above or below.

Flying low to make out signs on railroad stations
or other buildings is dangerous, yet sometimes has
to be done. I dare say that in time legislation will
make air marking compulsory everywhere, as it already is in Maryland, for instance, for towns with
more than 4000 inhabitants.   The Department of

Commerce suggests a uniform method of placing names near a railroad or close to a main highway for easy recognition. Large gas tanks are good places for signs, also. Once they are looked for in a definite location, they are more easily found from the air.

"My compass reads due west. I have been flying for more than an hour. Speed 100 m.p.h. In half an hour, if the course is correct and I have allowed properly for winds, I ought to cross a river which is fifty miles from Bugville. Beyond that river is a railroad track. The first town which appears to the left should be Prune City."

Wonder what a pilot thinks about? Well, something very much like that as he flies over unknown territory.

Crossing the continent I contrived to get myself lost, and not because of fog.

Flying west from Fort Worth I struck very bumpy weather. Air bumps act as do waves in a choppy sea, tossing one about. If severe, they make flying a small plane about like riding a couple of oceans in a canoe.

Through particularly bumpy going, while I tried to fly and also to pump gas from the reserve into the gravity tank, I lost my map. In that ship, it usually lay open upon my knee, fastened with a safety pin to my dress. But in the strenuous moments over Texas, the pin was somehow loosened and the map blew away.

When I had a chance to look about, there were

no landing marks with which to identify my location. So I decided to follow the same course that I had held over my last-known location, a little south of west.

Somewhat to the north, a highway with many busy cars soon became visible. I turned to fly beside that road. So many cars must be going somewhere, and I felt I would like to go there, too. In all the vast rolling country below, those automobiles were the only signs of life except an occasional ranch house or oil derrick at intervals of many miles. I chased that highway across the state into New Mexico, passing only a few unnamed towns, and then, with misgivings, I watched the cars scatter for their homes. The road and its traveling population simply oozed away, and I was left lonely and lost.

The sun began to sink. The purple haze of the dry countries rose on the horizon. I desired food. My plane desired gas, or would shortly. I wanted very much to get somewhere before dark.

A small cluster of houses grouped around an oil well, swam into the darkening landscape below me. Cautiously I circled low to see the condition of the ground, and the single wide flat .thoroughfare of the little community. Convinced that Main Street was the best visible place to land, I sat down at one end. At high altitudes where the air is thin, it is necessary to make a pretty fast landing, so I am afraid I broke speed ordinances as the Avro Avian rolled smartly through the heart of the city.

At once the community turned out to see who was in the plane, and I turned out to find where I was. My friendly metropolis claimed the age of six months, and the title of an oil boom town.

The citizens helped me fold the wings of the biplane and then, after sending telegrams by way of the single telephone, I dined at the Owl Café, from the much appreciated but invariable menu of fried eggs, coffee and bread. And the luxury of a real bed!

The coolness of that gorgeous high desert night was very grateful. Flying so much had caused a severe sunburn. For most of the journey, I wore a close fitting hat instead of the helmet which left a sunburned streak across my cheeks. Goggles cannot be abandoned on long hops, except in closed ships. They, of course, bequeath unburned rings of white around the eyes. In my log book I noted that when and if I reached Los Angeles, I should resemble a horned toad.

Down Main Street I took off the next morning, everyone helping me. Unfortunately in the preparations a thorn punctured one of my tires. While I enjoyed my morning eggs, the puncture was repaired. I thought, as I climbed aboard, that the tire was softening, but everyone said I was mistaken.

Then once more the billowing brown areas of the southwest stretched below me. Ocean flying is no more lonely than that over uncharted or uninhabited land. I was told that in about one hundred miles, in a somewhat southwesterly direction, there would be either a river with a railroad to the right, or a railroad main line with a highway on the left, depending on whether I was more west than south and vice versa.

You remember in your automobile touring the hazy rural directions sometimes given you? "About three, four miles down the road, turn to your left by an old barn, then across the creek—." At least in such cases you have a road to follow.

In this part of the west the rivers wriggle, cutting across country tortuously. I remember late that morning, when I came to a friendly railroad, I experienced much the feeling as did the *Friendship* crew in sighting land at the end of the transatlantic flight.

As I prepared to land at Pecos, I recalled the uncertainty of the repaired tire and sat down gingerly. The tire actually was flat but the light ship gave no trouble.

Pecos was very kind to me. Citizens repaired the stubborn tire and the Rotary Club, then in session, took me to luncheon. Starting that afternoon for El Paso came the first motor trouble of the trip, and I was forced down, landing among mesquite bushes and salt hills, in the best place—it was none too good—that I could see from 4000 feet.

It was near a road and cars gathered at once, the women seeming especially anxious to see what I looked like. Some day, I dare say, women can be flyers and yet not be regarded as curiosities!

As I was coming down, another plane passed and, with good air manners, circled about until the pilot saw that I was on the ground safely.

Airplanes are meant to fly, and it is sad to see one towed along the road. But it was my fate to see "G-EBUG" (my registration letters) thus return to Pecos. Because the wheels of the plane were not made for much rolling on the ground, we were forced to hold our pace to ten miles an hour and to stop every three miles to let the bearings cool. It was late and dark when the little ship was stowed behind a garage at Pecos, there to await new engine parts from El Paso.

It may not be all plain sailing, of course, if one chooses to step out informally over strange country visiting unfamiliar landing fields. But the fun of it is worth the price.

In regard to "G-EBUG"—these were the British license letters on Lady Heath's plane and I had left them when I purchased it from her. American licenses are combinations of letters and numbers, thus:

Those planes having an approved type certificate, commonly called an ATC, carry numerals prefixed by "C". This letter means the plane has passed tests for airworthiness prescribed by the Department of Commerce and may be flown anywhere in the U. S. A. When an "N" precedes the "C," it may be flown over foreign territory also. To illustrate, my own Lockheed license number is

NC 7952. Of course, all the planes on the airlines have a "C" license.

The Department also issues experimental licenses to be used on planes undergoing certain tests or being built. These numbers are preceded by an "X".

When a pilot changes any of the details of construction already approved by the Department of Commerce, he must notify an inspector and he then usually receives a restricted or "R" license, depending on the character of his alterations. Colonel Lindbergh's plane is an example for his number is NR 211.

With the increased number of airplanes to be licensed, the Department has lately been adding a division to the regular NC. Thus, the plane in which I established the first woman's speed record bore the number NC 497 H.

Now and then, a plane with numbers but no letters at all will be seen. That marking shows it cannot be licensed for some reason but is only identified. (G-EBUG and her kind, when first imported from England, bore only identification numbers.) Planes of the Department of Commerce all bear an S and are usually low numbers, NS 1, 2, 3, and so on.

"WHAT TO DO NEXT?"

IN the autumn of 1928, I returned from the little transcontinental jaunt. At Los Angeles I had visited the National Air Races of that year and renewed acquaintance with many friends, some of whom I had not seen since flying student days.

Now I was back in New York, ready to take up whatever the next job might be. Flying the Atlantic for some reason brought many offers of various types of work. Why such an expedition should fit one to go into a totally different occupation than any one has ever taken part in before, I have never comprehended. Offers from advertising agencies and other enterprises with which I was entirely unfamiliar came to me as they do to any other news figure of the moment. There were some opportunities to enter commercial aviation, too.

After Colonel Lindbergh's flight, the United States seemed to awake to the possibilities of air transportation. People spoke of it as a "coming thing," not realizing that commercial flying had been quietly developing for several years and that a network of airlines already existed. To many persons this expansion simply meant interest in aviation stocks and none in the possibility of their actually using airplanes for travel themselves.

Ray Long, guiding spirit of Cosmopolitan Magazine, asked me to join its staff as Aviation Editor. With "Cosmo's" enormous circulation I welcomed the opportunity to reach a great audience with my favorite subject. And in deciding to accept Mr. Long's offer, I knew that I was casting my lot permanently with aviation.

In addition to writing a series of articles, part of my time was spent answering the many letters which came, seeking information about various phases of flying. Just then, it seemed as if almost everyone wished to learn to fly. Certainly there was an enormous number of prospects. While I heard from many girls, just as many inquiries were made by boys, and men and women.

There were serious questions and foolish ones and those which told stories of poverty, ambition and dreams. An inventor had discovered a device which added thirty per cent to the efficiency of any plane. A real estate man wished to enter aviation because it provided a "future." A young chap wrote, "Give me the name of a school of aviation. I'm only an office boy, but I'm a darn good one." Teachers, mechanics, laborers,—an endless throng seemed to pass my desk.

Scrawled on yellow paper in pencil, a youngster asked, "Why is the monoplane more faster than the biplane?" And that was hard to answer in a few words for a child.

"Dear Miss Earhart," ran one letter, "I have quarreled with my boy friend and have decided to take up aviation. Please tell me how."

I confess I was puzzled with the sequence of events. Had the writer cheerfully thrown over her admirer in order to fly, or did she think to "end it all" in an airplane? I couldn't guess, so told her, as I did all others who asked "how", that the first step in learning to fly is to pass the physical examination given by the Department of Commerce.

I have been congratulated for swimming the English Channel, and being picked up by a ship near the Azores. So I received a few inquiries meant either for Gertrude Ederle or Ruth Elder (Camp, now). I have always felt that the three of us were somewhat thoughtless to have names all beginning with E.

One of my most frequent questions was, "Do you know Colonel Lindbergh?" Many had to do with sensations. How did it feel to fly high or low or fast or at all? Then there was one surprise package which does not surprise me any more. It was wrapped thus—and still is: "I am *tremendously* interested in aviation. I have always *longed* to go up in a plane but never had the chance. It must be *wonderful* to sail about in the blue sky." Surprise. "Will you please send me your autograph?"

"My mother won't let me fly." In one form or another that was a plaint I heard many times.

In the early months of my editorship I evolved a list of "don'ts" for prospective flyers' parents. Here they are:—do you want to try them on yours?

Don't issue edicts against flying until you know something about it from experience.

Don't let your children fly in any but a licensed government-inspected plane.

Don't, if they want to learn to fly themselves, allow them to attend any but the best schools, about whose equipment and personnel you are thoroughly informed.

Don't, if they are to have a plane of their own, be penny wise and pound foolish. If necessary, wait until you or they can afford to buy adequate motors and demonstratedly established craft, rather than run the tragic risks of false economies and short cuts.

Don't let the boy or girl hurry his or her training.

Don't let anyone consider flying seriously until he or she has a thorough and satisfactory medical examination.

Don't try to tell the instructor how to do the training.

Don't fail to back the youngster who has begun to fly, with your full confidence; don't worry him by your worry.

The main needs is to avoid "bootleg" flying— doing it secretly because parents object. I am sure some mothers and fathers do not know how often their youngsters find a way to visit air fields. Anyone who is situated so that he can observe any flying activities, knows there are always children and young men and women in the background watching what goes on. They line the surrounding fences, if any, and they invade factories and hangars and transport waiting rooms whenever they can. They want to know all about airplanes and their operation, and most of all, they want to fly. Often they will go up for a free ride with any old pilot in any old airplane if given the opportunity. Or if parents have issued an unreasonable "Thou shalt not fly," they will save their money and very naturally buy the cheapest trip available—which may or may not be the safest.

Now there is safe flying and that which is unsafe—exactly as there is safe or unsafe driving or boating. Parents, one or the other or both, should go with their children on the first ride. To see that the safeguards of a licensed pilot and licensed plane are in force is just as definitely a responsibility as overseeing other present-day activities. For the present generation is going to get off the earth some way or other!

Putting off doesn't solve the problems of aviation. I have had mothers say to me, "I shall let my daughter fly when she is sixteen." (Or eighteen or some other age, determined I don't know how.)

"Why not now?" I have queried, only to be given funny or interesting but seldom adequate, answers. Sometimes I knew Daughter had already been up, so the explanation did not matter anyway.

Needless to say, I regret the necessity for this lack of cooperation, just as I do when parents without investigation forbid boys and girls to pursue subjects in college leading to an aeronautical career. That work may be the one field in which the young person may have the greatest aptitude, and it seems a pity to try to force him or her into another.

I have been rather severe on the parents in the foregoing. Perhaps I should turn to another im-

Three vice-presidents in the early days of the
Ludington Line—Gene Vidal, A.E. and Paul F. Collins

In the cockpit of her Lockheed-Vega

portant class of adults—and talk about teachers.
They, the women and men who are shaping the
women and men of tomorrow—give me a special
urge to make at least one flight compulsory for all
pedagogues.

In my magazine work I had letters from college
students asking how to persuade deans to permit
flying. In contrast to the liberality of some institutions, there was absolute ban on it in others. This
even went so far as forbidding travel by air between
home and campus, on penalty of expulsion. Of
course, in some instances, there was a great deal to
say for the dean's point of view. In one university
an accident, due to carelessness, as I remember it,
had occurred with the result that discipline too lax
there before had been tightened unreasonably. All
flying was taboo.

To my mind the sensible middle course, at college as anywhere else, is to have supervised flying.
A plane may be misused or mishandled and its
safety characteristics abused, as may be those of
any other vehicle.

My correspondence convinced me that young
people today are increasingly accepting aviation as
a matter of course. To the newer generation a
plane isn't much more unusual than an automobile.
When they talk aviation, they are apt to know what
they are talking about.

Speaking of this modern attitude, I landed for
a night once in a small town in New Mexico. There
was no landing field or any sort of facility for

planes. I learned later that none had been there for years. Scarcely had my wheels come to rest, when a boy on a bicycle arrived. He eyed my little Avian. "Huh, you haven't got slots, have you?" he inquired. The child had had no opportunity to become acquainted with this development except through reading, yet he not only recognized my plane as one often equipped with slots, but knew what these gadgets looked like.

Aviation chatter is routine. The modern vocabulary is studded with "ailerons", "r.p.m.'s", "slips", "stalls", "dead sticks", and the like. Among other things, aviation is making its contribution to the language. Some of its uncommon phrases of to-day will be common enough tomorrow. And conversely, certain landlubber words of now may be seldom heard in the future.

AVIATION AS IT IS

THE privileges of writing and flying were not the only heritage of the Atlantic Flight. Business beckoned, too, and to me "business" meant commercial aviation, as I have said before.

I had entered the scene when the industry was boiling with new enterprises. Even when the first sizeable passenger lines started, neither the operators nor the traveling public quite knew what it was all about. Aviation certainly had to be "sold" and the operators leaned to the notion that a luxury service was what the public wanted. Thus, the advertising of the period carried descriptions of the amenities to be found in flying.

"Interior decorations and fittings are in soft restful tones with here and there a touch of modern art. For the most part interiors have been designed to harmonize with the natural colors of the country along the route. A wall lamp is above the seat of each passenger and an indirect ceiling light brightens the entire cabin on dark days."

I think there were several good reasons for this publicity policy. First, it informed people that riding in airplanes was not materially different from travel by other means. By making the trappings of aviation as familiar as possible, timid souls were the more easily persuaded to climb aboard.

"Why, they can serve meals in those big planes; they have parcel racks like trains; passengers can read—surely they can't be so bad." This was about the thought process hoped for. Second, it seemed logical to stress the point that air travel would not be so unpleasant as the majority of airports looked. And last, but not least, the high fares in effect at the time had to be justified in the eyes of prospective patrons. The more one pays for a car, the more nickel trimming one expects!

My next step, then, was to join one of the pioneer passenger lines, Transcontinental Air Transport, in the traffic department. My job was to sell flying to women, both by talking about it and by watching details of handling passengers, which were calculated to appeal to feminine travelers. Justly or unjustly, air ticket sellers accused women of being the greatest sales resistance encountered. They wouldn't go up themselves, said these men, and they wouldn't let their families do so. One phrased it, "Father won't fly, if Mother says he can't."

In my work, I did considerable flying over the Line on the regular transports, and in addition fulfilled my speaking engagements here and there, the country over, in my own plane. On these flights I sometimes took my mother with me. To her, flying became so commonplace that she took along a detective story in order to keep awake when we were in the air for long periods.

With the very rapid development of aviation, a

new attitude on the part of the traveling public entered the picture. Airlines began to be accepted as a necessity, like railroads and bus lines. Increasingly it became apparent that there was a need for frequency of service and lowered fares. Airplanes sometimes offered no advantages over ground facilities in time saving, if they didn't fly often enough to be a convenience to passengers. For instance, a man who wished, say, to go to Cleveland from New York might find a plane left for the west once a day at nine o'clock in the morning. If he couldn't leave until noon, he could make better time by taking a train that night and arriving at Cleveland about the time the next plane was leaving from New York. But the operators couldn't be expected to put on a heavy schedule to accommodate only a few customers. To reach enough to justify several additional trips a day, it was obvious fares had to be reduced.

While some operators were engrossed with the problem of the long haul, others, equally pioneering, studied those of shorter routes at higher speeds. In Transcontinental Air Transport, I came to know Gene Vidal and Paul Collins, both members of that organization. Collins, who was superintendent of operations, had been a famous air mail flyer with, as I remember it, 8000 hours to his credit. A great pilot himself, he understood the background of airplanes and other pilots.

Vidal, an ex-army flyer and engineer, had been on the technical staff of T. A. T. His interest and experience chiefly concerned the analysis of problems of passenger carrying and operation costs. At West Point he had been selected for the all-American football team, had established track records which still hold there, and was a member of several Olympic teams. He also contrived to play baseball and basketball.

Of Collins and his varied flying career many stories are told. His nickname, by the way, is "Dog"—for some reason. I once asked him whether he'd ever had to use a parachute.

"Yes, I'm a caterpillar", he admitted.

"How did it happen?", I inquired.

"Well," he answered, "years ago when I was flying the night mail between New York and Cleveland, I got into a bad storm." Then he described how, in the buffeting that ensued, a wing came off his plane. At first he didn't know what had happened, as he could not see outside the cockpit. But in a second he realized he would have to jump. Cutting off the motor, he bailed out and waited for his chute to open. Very shortly it did—clear of the disabled ship he had just left.

An exquisite feeling of relief surged over him as he found himself safe and sound several thousand feet above the crowd. When he jumped, he was over a heavily wooded section of Pennsylvania. As he settled down through the darkness, a thought suddenly struck him which spoiled his entire journey earthward. His relief of a few moments before was replaced by anxiety.

"I certainly was worried," Collins admitted.

"I'll *bet* you were," I agreed. "You might have been heading for a house or a bunch of trees or a lake. It wouldn't be much fun to come down when you couldn't see what was underneath."

"Well, I didn't mind that so much," said the "Dog," "but I got to worrying about meeting a bear when I landed. I had heard from more enthusiastic hunters than I, that there were a lot of them in that section."

As it happened, he landed in a clearing unhurt and saw no bears. Just the same, he says, he hopes he won't have to jump again—in that region.

Vidal and Collins had ideas of their own about airlines. In due course, they left T. A. T. and interested Philadelphia capital in the establishment of a different sort of operation between New York and Washington. It was to be an hourly service with ten round trips a day, the first of its kind ever attempted over such a distance.

The plans were really daring when it is remembered that this two-hundred-mile stretch is as well served by ground transportation as is any in the world. "You won't get people into airplanes when they have such good service on trains or buses," was the warning heard most frequently in the preliminary period. However, the organization went forward with the most minute details of cost and administration worked out in advance. As unusual as the original plan was the fact that all cost estimates came true!

I was asked to join the project and gladly did so, becoming with Vidal and Collins, a vice-president of the corporation when it was launched. I had the fun of sitting in on all the details of actual commercial air pioneering, first on paper and later in practise.

From nothing at all Vidal and Collins created the organization they wanted and administered it later. The result was something new in air transport. With the exception of an air ferry service over San Francisco Bay, it was the first really frequent service in the world. There were no frills about it. The aim was to carry passengers quickly and cheaply at regular intervals between three important centers—the railroad principle of service applied to air travelers.

The line became a real success, to the surprise of many aeronautical experts who had not believed that passenger carrying without government help in the form of mail contracts could pay its way. In the first year 66,279 passengers were carried and 1,523,400 miles flown. The daily totals exceed, by the way, the combined totals of the various lines flying from London to Paris—a distance about the same as from New York to Washington. I think most Americans don't realize how far aviation in their own country has outstripped that of England and the continent, despite the longer period of the service abroad.

There are more passengers carried every twenty-four hours, as well as mail, in the United States than in all of Europe combined. The service is as good, if not better, the planes generally faster, and safety records the same as for France, Germany and England. Rates in this country tend to approximate railroad plus Pullman fares. Do you know that every twenty-four hours planes on schedule fly at least 150,000 miles? Nor does that total include the uncounted thousands of miles flown by private owners and in army and navy manœuvers. At that, commercial aviation is just beginning to get ready to start.

As with T. A. T., my duties in the New York, Philadelphia and Washington Airway primarily concerned passengers—getting them, and pacifying them when things went wrong. There were endless letters to be answered, and many many speeches to audiences of various kinds. Always my talks were about flying from one point of view or another. During this period of vocal salesmanship, I met college girls, women's clubs, professional groups and mixtures of these, as well as all sorts and conditions of men before whom I also spoke.

Usually I asked those in the audiences who had flown to raise their hands. In the metropolitan areas among the women, the professional groups led in the number who had been in the air. Further, nearly all who had not seemed quite willing to go when opportunity offered. As an example of this progressive spirit, I myself ferried four mem-

bers of the Philadelphia Club of Advertising
Women (all my plane could accommodate) to a
national convention in Washington. The members
simply preferred to go by air. At the time, I could
not help contrasting their attitude with the reputa-
tion the ticket sellers had accorded women a year
or two before.

To return to the airline, there were minor problems always cropping up, having to do with the
comfort and convenience of passengers. I soon
learned the truth of the old axiom that a pleased
customer seldom takes the trouble to say he was
well served—it is the disgruntled one who takes
pen in hand and writes and writes and writes.

Temperatures in the planes were too high or too
low; the bumpiness of the air was the *Company's*
fault. Periodically the matter of baggage came
up. With a railroad where weight doesn't count
for much, the individual may have any number of
bags and bundles. But in a plane thirty pounds,
or one medium-sized piece of luggage, is the usual
allowance unless excess is paid. Even then in a
crowded plane the Department of Commerce limits
must not be exceeded. (Just as on the ground one
may not overload trucks on the highways.)

One day a man with thirteen pieces turned up.
Maybe the number had nothing to do with it, but it
proved bad luck for him as well as for us.

"Your excess charge for this will amount to just
about another fare," said the dispatcher who
weighed it.

"What?" exclaimed the passenger. "Another fare? Why, I can take all the baggage I wish on trains and no questions asked."

"Sorry," replied the dispatcher. "We have to make this charge. Weight is very important in airplanes."

"Well, I won't pay, and I'll have my money back on my reservation. Railroads don't make such silly rules as airlines."

"Ask the gent," said a voice in the crowd, "if he ever tried to take a trunk into a parlor car."

As the seat had been reserved for Mr. Thirteen, and the plane was about to start, the refund was necessarily refused. Needless to say, however, considerable correspondence on "silly rules" resulted.

On the line, we carried some express and odd packages of all kinds. I, myself, chaperoned a canary from New York to Washington. The bird appeared much more frightened in the air than some of the other animals that patronized us!

One of these was a pony. For some reason or other, there was a rush about getting him from Philadelphia to the capital. So he was sold two seats (although he had to stand partly in the aisle) and made the voyage very comfortably. To prove he really flew, he had his picture taken wearing a pair of goggles as he alighted.

Dogs, mostly diminutive breeds, were constant passengers. Theoretically no pets were allowed. However, it was surprising at the end of the ride

how many demi-tasse dogs emerged from the shel-
tering coats and furs of innocent looking feminine
voyagers.

When passengers were frank about animals, the
rules were occasionally stretched. One day a
woman called to say she just had to take a dog from
Washington to New York. Could she, please?
"It's a lap dog," she added, "—my dearest possession."

Everyone has heard tales of large over-aged
children whose parents attempt to pass them off as
under the half fare limit on trains and buses. Airlines have also learned to know the variation of that
little act, but the first time the part was played by
a dog, it was a surprise.

When the woman of the telephone call arrived,
followed by what onlookers described as a young
heifer, the men at the airport felt they had been
betrayed.

"You'll have to hold him on your lap, Madame,"
said one, eyeing him coldly. "Otherwise, he can't
go." With an expression of some dismay, the passenger boarded the plane and sat down underneath
the dog. I think he enjoyed the trip more than
she did.

Of course, the operators made their share of mistakes. One day, a Fifth Avenue florist, wishing
to demonstrate the perfection of air transportation,
sent a magnificent box of violets to a client in
Washington. The messenger unfortunately stored
the precious package on the heater and its contents

on arrival looked like spinach decorated with silver ribbons.

Some ice cream met a somewhat similar fate. A manufacturer in New York was to supply the dessert for a luncheon in Philadelphia. At nine o'clock the packed boxes were put aboard at Newark Airport, and the plane left on schedule. Unfortunately someone forgot to remove them at the Philadelphia stop and they went merrily on to Washington. There they were held while inquiries were made up and down the line as to where they belonged. After some delay, they started back to Philadelphia. I do not know just what subsequent travels the ice cream made, but about six thirty it turned up in a liquid state at the place where the luncheon had been—mute testimony to airline efficiency.

The most routine blunder, at least in the beginning, was to sell the same seat to two persons. When eleven passengers appear at the last moment for a ten place plane there is an element of embarrassment.

With the New York, Philadelphia and Washington Airway, as with all others, weather really held the whip hand. Under certain conditions it is impossible to fly, as I have explained. When planes had to remain on the ground, schedules were cancelled and passengers reluctantly turned over to the railroads.

However, the bugaboo of weather is being progressively overcome. Experiments are continuously being made to improve instruments for blind flying, and a system of weather reporting and forecasting has been developed to help meet flyers' needs.

For instance, at stated intervals every hour the United States Weather Bureau gives a report of conditions to the various localities along the established airways. Any airport can be equipped with a teletype to get this service.

Not only is weather information available by teletype but it is broadcast every hour, as well. Thus, any pilot in the air who has proper radio equipment can tune in on a specified wave length and learn exactly what conditions prevail in his territory. What he hears aloft can be listened to on the ground, of course. These broadcasts, by the way, are given out verbally and not in code. At many fields they are amplified with loud speakers so that they are easily heard by everyone concerned.

In addition to the weather bureau service, whose distribution for the airways is handled by the Department of Commerce, several of the large air transport companies have supplementary service of their own. Their pilots in the air are in constant touch with their control stations and with other pilots, while special reports are received at intervals from observers at key positions adjacent to the route.

"DOC" KIMBALL

THE man upon whom every house-party hostess depends, the man whose advice is sought by promoters of prize-fights and Salvation Army picnics and upon whose words farmers wait eagerly, their thoughts on corn and wheat, is the weather man. And there is a special guiding genius upon whose accurate information the lives of flyers often depend. It is as important to know what he says, as to know that a motor isn't missing.

The guide, meteorological philosopher and friend of all flyers—the man who has had his hand in all the major flights originating in this country—does not fly himself.

But it is he who says "Go" to those who do.

"What's the weather? What does Dr. Kimball say?"

That double-barreled question was asked countless times during the thirteen weary days at Trepassey about which I have told you, as we poised on the verge of the transatlantic flight.

Returning to New York afterward, I met the "weather man" on whom we had so depended. I found him a middle aged person with a mop of grey hair topping a broad brow. He had friendly eyes, a thoughtful smile and a low, soft, southern drawling voice. The first thing he wanted to know was about the meteorological conditions met with on the flight.

"When you have time—when you get through with this," he said, indicating the crowd, "please tell me some day exactly what you encountered on the flight. After all, we're able really to find out so little about over-ocean weather—and evidently what we predicted didn't pan out."

One day I visited Dr. Kimball at the Weather Bureau perched up at the top of the Whitehall Building in lower New York City. It was mid morning. Dr. Kimball stood at a high desk, and as we talked, the periodic delivery of telegraph flimsies interrupted our conversation. These messages contained cabalistic figures from Manitoba, Kansas or Cuba, recording conditions at that particular point—the barometric pressure, wind direction and velocity, visibility and temperature, and whether rain, snow, fog or sunshine prevailed.

On the desk before him lay an outline map of the United States and the Atlantic. As the information trickled in, Dr. Kimball penciled swirling lines across it. In final form each swirl outlined specific pressure areas. Little pools and wide eddies of these lines, called isobars, gradually covered the paper, while on a companion map developed another picture puzzle of isotherms, lines designating temperatures.

Dr. Kimball and I talked of the interesting phenomena of weather movement—for it is the calculation of movement which is the basis of meteorological prediction. The "highs" and "lows" (that is, fair weather and storm centers) are seldom static

Looking down on an aircraft carrier

Where the Wrights first flew—Orville Wright, Senator
Hiram Bingham and A.E. at Kitty Hawk, N.C.

for long. Almost universally they move from west to east in the United States, just as prevailing winds on this hemisphere and over the Atlantic are westerly, primarily controlled by the revolution of the earth itself.

Each storm center, Dr. Kimball explained, revolves in a counter clockwise direction, when it is north of the equator.

"Have you ever noticed," he asked, "how water draining from a basin always swirls opposite the hands of a clock?"

"We're usually through with the weather map about noon," Dr. Kimball went on. "Generally these reports come in from one hundred and fifty stations in the United States. Then there are thirty or more from Canada, and others from Bermuda, and from several points in the arctic, including Greenland. In the summer we get regular reports from the ice patrol up in the Grand Banks region. And, of course, each morning the data come from Great Britain covering the eastern Atlantic and Europe."

It takes about four hours to compile and digest all this far-flung information. Once in, and the weather map made, the bureau is ready to issue its predictions. That "Fair and Warmer" prophecy you read in the paper isn't at all the guesswork of some individual optimist; it's the product of the labor of a hundred men or more, and its compilation has cost thousands of dollars.

The ground hog and the "nature signs" of the

amateur weather prophet are losing out in the demand for accurate information. Modern economics can't depend on them. Long flights and important business ventures which need fair weather must have better foundation than:

> Mackerel in the sky,
> Three days dry.

"How many ships report ocean weather information?" I asked.

"Not nearly so many as we need," Dr. Kimball sighed. "We haven't adequate appropriation yet for all the service we'd like, but it's much better than it used to be. The storms over the North Atlantic are larger than any known on land, extending sometimes in one vast disturbance from Newfoundland to the British Isles. That is the extent—how high they are, we do not know.

"During the hurricane season a hundred or more ships in West Indian waters report. If vessels in the North sent regular data, our over-ocean weather maps should be pretty efficient. That's important for maritime commerce, and of course essential in the development of transatlantic flying. Also such information would help us tremendously in forecasting weather conditions on shore, both for our own continent and for Europe."

Dr. Kimball, like so many others, believes that regular transatlantic air service, whether by dirigibles or airplanes, is inevitable—and near. As a matter of fact, one of the barriers to it today is lack

of complete weather information. Not that airplanes are frail craft and can't ride out a storm, but
that they are so peculiarly competent to take advantage of meteorological opportunities and avoid hazards.

A ship has to plow on its course, whatever the
storm conditions. Aircraft may sometimes dodge
a storm or adverse wind by flying at an altitude at
which conditions are favorable. For instance, almost always if a high enough altitude is attained,
the wind is westerly in our latitude, whatever its
direction on the ground.

In his book "Skyward," Commander Byrd says:
"I now think that the *America* (his transatlantic
Fokker monoplane) could conquer almost any
storms that might be met in crossing the Atlantic.
The only ocean condition that need be serious for
the planes of the future is the hurricane, which
might exhaust the fuel supply."

He speaks of the planes of today. Large, they
are, many of them weighing tons. What the size
and weight and strength of the aircraft of tomorrow will be, is guesswork.

Most experienced pilots agree with him. And
Byrd, remember, is speaking *after* an Atlantic
crossing. Before he flew, the Weather Bureau gave
him the best information possible. He required a
westerly wind to push him toward his goal and thus
augment his fuel supply. Even with the sketchy
data available, he got what was promised him—
though there were unexpected conditions thrown

in, as later happened in Chamberlin's great flight to
Germany, and with our own *Friendship* Flight.

The time is at hand when meteorological experts
will be able to hand a pilot a weather map of the
Atlantic upon which the locations of barometric
highs and lows will be plotted exactly, both for the
moment and say, twelve hours thence. Already
the Hydrographic Office issues monthly charts of
the upper air, with a notice in the corner reading,

"Recommended Transatlantic Airplane Route: In the
selection of the routes shown on the charts, the northern-
most route which appears practicable in view of distances,
temperatures, favorability of wind, and general weather
information, gleaned from analyses of recent transoceanic
flights and the present development of aviation, the route
from the Azores to Plymouth, England, is the route recommended for the month."

In Dr. Kimball's office in New York, the inquiries concerning weather run a wide gamut, those
directly concerning aviation being yet in the
minority.

"I am trying to get some coal across the river,
and the ice keeps piling up against the docks. Can
you tell me when the wind will change so I can get
the shipment out?"

"Isn't the U. S. A. going to have any snow this
year? I can't go to Canada every time I want to
ski."

"Can you tell me, please, whether it's going to
rain this afternoon? I want to know about wearing rubbers."

Fifteen hundred times a day over the phone come similar questions, some comic, some—or what lies behind them—tragic. Even though there are fewer of them, those concerning flying weather come frequently enough. However, with the establishment of weather bureaus on the airways, most of the spot news type of inquiry go directly to the airport offices.

Dr. Kimball takes transatlantic flights seriously. During the preparations for several of the hops, I know he stayed up night after night, coordinating the data that came in, and giving to the fliers and their associates the best he could. I really think that he did not go to bed at all during the thirteen days when the *Friendship* remained at Trepassey.

When George Haldeman and Ruth Elder started out, Dr. Kimball had told them they would meet a storm near the Azores. They took the chance of running through it, however, rather than wait until a coming storm, then recorded in the Middle West, should sweep eastward across the country and make the fields here at New York impossible for a take-off. With the heavy load of gasoline, the wheels of the plane would have bogged down on a rainsoaked runway.

That particular hazard is eliminated, as far as New York is concerned now, for an airport with 3000 feet runways which don't become soft in rain, has since been finished.

Weather, in Dr. Kimball's belief, also figured in the loss of Hinchcliffe, who started to fly the Atlantic from east to west. He put to sea with favorable northeast winds, but subsequently, it became evident later, encountered areas of falling barometer in mid-Atlantic, with freezing temperature that may well have weighted his plane with ice.

Dr. Kimball told me, too, what happened when Admiral Byrd started for France. At Cape Race, the easternmost point of Newfoundland, a barometer recorded fair weather. But hourly reports from a vessel heading westward on the steamer lane recorded a steadily falling barometer. Apparently a storm lay across its course, which was also Byrd's.

At midnight just off Cape Race, the final message came from the steamer. The reading of its barometer was far lower than that of the barometer ashore. At once the meteorologist, studying all the available data in his New York office, realized that the ship's barometer was inaccurate—that actually there was no storm on the first leg of the journey.

"The start of that Byrd flight was the most dramatic of all," Dr. Kimball told me. "When I told him of the adverse prospects for the next day, he went to sleep. He was staying with a friend on Long Island, not far from Roosevelt Field. When at midnight we ran down this mistake of barometric readings, the whole map changed.

"I phoned Byrd, and told him it looked pretty hopeful for the following winds he needed. Then I worked out the weather map as quickly as I could and drove out to him. We got there about two o'clock and went over the situation.

1911 – a Burgess-Wright biplane lands and takes off

1931 – a Pitcairn autogiro lands and takes off

" 'We'll go,' said Byrd.

"The *America's* crew joined the Commander at Roosevelt Field, where the ship was already warming up at the top of the incline they had built to get a running start. Just as dawn broke through low clouds, it started to rain.

" 'Is this rain serious?' Byrd asked me.

"I told him the data showed at worst a light local shower, and advised that he go ahead. He went. And, as you know, the heavily loaded *America* took off just before they reached the end of the runway."

So the start of Admiral Byrd's great flight— "the prettiest piece of navigation you could imagine," Dr. Kimball calls it—hinged entirely on weather data. I am sure that the weather man who started him on his way slept not at all until Byrd was safely in France.

To show how much he is appreciated, "Doc" Kimball was asked to be a Guest of Honor at a dinner given by those who had participated in all heavier than air transatlantic flights. Of course, not all could come, but among those who did, were Chamberlin, Balchen, Byrd, Lindbergh, Yancy, Assolant (who came from France to be present) and Courtney. Ruth Elder and I were the women included among these flying folk.

In winter crossings, many a ship is delayed by weather. Even with railroads, periodically snow-slides or washouts hold the whip hand. On country roads, mud and snow may upset the best made automobile plans, and every city dweller knows the traffic congestion that follows a swift and heavy snowstorm. Weather again!

Yes, the state of weather has a hand in making or marring many human activities, ranging from crop raising to transportation.

The establishment of weather bureaus began with the "Crimean Storm" of 1854. Sweeping across the Black Sea, it sank many ships at Balaklava, which carried food and necessities for the besiegers of Sebastopol, during the bitter winter.

The loss of the French Warship *Henry IV* in this disaster led the astronomer Leverrier, Director of the National Observatory at Paris, to trace the course of the storm across Europe from west to east. The outcome of this study was the establishment by the French Government of the first system of weather reporting. From it ultimately developed the service of storm warning and weather forecasting that now exists throughout the world.

Since then, the science of applied meteorology has steadily progressed—with aviation presenting its newest problem. In this clearly developing period it seems to me women might well be interesting themselves in becoming meteorologists, work interesting in itself and an opportunity to become acquainted with aviation. So far as I can find out, there are very very few who are preparing to do so.

"Is there any reason why women cannot be 'weather men'?" I asked the head of one of the large weather bureau offices not long ago.

"Well, no," he said, "except that they would

have to go out in bad weather sometimes and climb ladders to collect data and make observations."

Had I not known about civil service examinations, I might have received the impression that wearing overalls well was a requirement for women in meteorology. However, to be sure that entrance opportunities were about the same for both sexes I asked about examinations.

"Yes. Candidates can be either men or women. Usually the head of a department has the privilege of choosing which one he prefers when passing grades are about the same."

"Are there any women at all in the Weather Bureau?" was my next question.

"A few—mostly at Washington, D. C. Their positions are classified as stenographic and clerical though most of those in the latter are really minor observers. Of course, there are many more in the first division."

While most Weather Bureau women may be in Washington, I know of one observer who is stationed on a regular airway, or, rather, an airway runs by the place she lives.

Just where the Hudson narrows at Peekskill, there stands St. Mary's Academy. Fog often lingers longest in that region and forms more quickly. Pilots on the New York-Albany run know if they can get past there, they can usually reach either terminal. Sister Mary Anthony at stated intervals sends in a full meteorological report, so that they may know the weather at that important point.

EXPERIMENTING AGAIN

AFTER the airline was organized and comfortably operating, it was time for me again to do some flying of my own and such experimenting as opportunity might offer.

Just then the autogiro was the very newest thing in aviation, and so naturally enough I found myself drawn toward it.

Probably no other recent aeronautical development has created the interest it has, among engineers and laymen alike. Miles (I'm sure) of words concerning it have appeared in newspapers and magazines. In fact, so much space has been assigned its doings that I am at a loss to know how or where to start another biography. Perhaps if I begin at the beginning, I may find some bit of information not told a hundred times already.

Perhaps the public's unusually great interest in it is conditioned by its promise of greater safety to the inexperienced flyer. Perhaps the very strangeness of its design is responsible for the great interest displayed in it wherever it makes an appearance.

Curiously, the history of the autogiro starts in a book. Before ever a model of one was made, a portly volume had been written about it. Under the title, *The Theory of Autorotation,* a young Spanish mathematician had described the habits

A.E. and her "flying billboard"

Louise Thaden

and character of a paddle-winged airplane which had never existed.

Juan de la Cierva was the name of the author, and he was a thoughtful, adventurous, inventive person, with an abiding interest in flying and flying machines. He really came to invent the autogiro because of an airplane accident. One day, at a local airdrome, he had witnessed a crack-up in landing. Though no one was hurt the incident convinced him that aviation would never amount to much unless some of its hazards were removed. The hazard he thought of particularly was that due to fast landings. Coming in at express train speeds, as is necessary in most planes, was to him a serious barrier to future progress. He, therefore, calmly set out to do what no one else had been able to do— think out a contraption which should possess high speed in flight and low speed, with control, in landing.

I cannot say how he evolved his theory nor how long it took him. But a story is told of him after he finished. Gathering up the sheets covered with abstruse formulas, he handed them to an engineer friend and said,

"Now *you* build it."

It is not to be inferred from that remark that Señor Cierva leaves the problems of construction entirely to others. On the contrary, for the dozen years that autogiros have been struggling in their present state of development, he has been actively connected with these details. Further, I imagine he will continue to be so until their mechanical perfection more closely approaches his theory.

For it must be remembered that the autogiro is still an experimental airplane. To compete commercially with the other type it still must increase its cruising speed to more than its present eighty miles an hour, carry a larger load on less horsepower than now required, and carry more than two hours' fuel supply. It must become lower in cost and upkeep, too, to appeal to the private owner who wants a plane he can treat as he does his car.

But such faults will doubtless be overcome as the autogiro grows up. And already it can do many of the things its inventor dreamed of. Like a bird it can settle to earth and stop—with no roll at all on the ground. A passenger I took up once described this characteristic very aptly by saying, as he got out,

"Well, she lands just like a turkey buzzard."

The "buzzard" landing obviously requires much less space than does the long roll of conventional fast planes. As would be imagined, the autogiro can get off in less space, too, and climb more steeply than many straight winged craft.

A picturesque example of its ability to land in small spaces was afforded last year when Jim Ray brought one down on the south lawn of the White House, an occasion on which the Collier Trophy was presented to its manufacturers in America. Curiously it was a more historic occasion than most people were aware of. Few remembered

—certainly it was in none of the press reports I saw—that a plane had landed in exactly the same place twenty years before. That was when Harry N. Atwood flew a 30 h.p. Burgess-Wright biplane into the White House grounds on July 14, 1911, when he was presented by President Taft with a gold medal given by the Aero Club of Washington.

There should be use for giros as sportsmen pilots' planes where large airports are not convenient. A smooth pasture or extra sized back yard should suffice for ordinary hopping up and down. Too, they may find a use as ferries about crowded city areas, where airline terminals because of high land values, are situated far from the business centers. Passengers may transfer to a waiting taxi-giro and be deposited much nearer their destination than the transport liners could bring them. By the way, whenever in-town landings are discussed, the possibility of making them on roofs of buildings is brought up. It might be of interest to note that finding sufficient space is not the greatest problem. In most large cities area enough could be found. The real difficulty is the eddying of air currents in the canyons of the streets, which may adversely affect all types of aircraft when landing, dirigibles, airplanes and 'giros.

I have spoken of autogiros on one hand and conventional airplanes on the other. I do not wish to give the impression that the former are not airplanes because they apparently have no wings. Such is not strictly true. As everyone knows, Mr.

Cierva's brain children have four blades which revolve above the pilot's head. When these are going fast enough for a flight (a hundred or more times a minute) they constitute a round wing. So that instead of being lifted by a rectangular surface, as in most planes, the autogiro sails along on a large pie plate, so to speak. The small wing, with the upturned tips, underneath the rotor blades, does not help much in supporting the weight of the plane in the air. Its duty is more to provide certain stability and hold the ailerons. Of course, the principle of the rotating wing type airplane, which is the family name of the autogiro, is not quite so simple as this description may sound. But regarded in this way, these craft may seem less of freaks than they look.

Now let me tell you of my first flight. It took place near Philadelphia on a bright spring day.

Jim Ray, chief test pilot and vice-president of one of the companies which builds autogiros, took me up for fifteen or twenty minutes around the field. He made a couple of landings and then brought his giro to a stop.

"Now," said he, climbing out, "you take it up."

"Aren't you going to give me any dual instruction?" I asked blankly. "I've had only a few minutes ride in this craft, as a passenger, you know."

"That's all right," he smiled reassuringly. "You'll get along. Just remember everything I've told you."

Everything he'd told me! I tried to remember one single thing, as I realized I was being invited to solo without so much as trying a landing or take-off myself.

I looked at the rotors over my head and the unfamiliar gadgets before me on the instrument board and I began to feel exactly as I had when I made my first solo in any airplane eleven years before.

Mr. Ray stood beside the autogiro, unbuckling his parachute.

"I'll wait for you here," he said, indicating a small hillock in the landing field.

"Just what my first instructor said," I thought to myself, and wondered that his words should so fit the present situation. For here I was a novice again, with all of the uncertainty of a beginner.

No other person has had so many autogiro hours as Jim Ray. He knows more about the habits of the whirligigs than anyone but the inventor. No wonder I felt self-conscious in his presence!

Thinking over the moment when the autogiro rose into the air, I am at a loss now to say whether I flew it or it flew me. I only know that suddenly I found myself peering down upon some tree tops and sailing along merrily over a country road almost before I was aware "we" had hopped off.

But it doesn't take long to become used to the autogiro, if it is handled like a regular airplane. I found that out when I came in for the first landing. I also found out there are many tricks to learn, if one wishes to get out of it, all that it is capable of.

For experts can make giros do seemingly easy stunts that novices couldn't possibly duplicate—a truism which holds good for any skilled pastime.

After I had played with the autogiro for several hours at different times, I was given the chance to try an altitude hop. No one knew exactly how high a stock model could climb. So it was suggested that I take one upstairs and keep on going until it would go no farther. The "ceiling" of an airplane is as much performance data as speed. Automobile, motor boat and airplane manufacturers all find it valuable to check theoretical calculations with practical demonstrations.

Even though simple in itself, any official test requires more preparation than might be supposed. For instance, a representative of the National Aeronautic Association in Washington must be called to install the barograph. This instrument registers altitude and also shows the time consumed on the flight as recorded on a revolving drum. The barograph must be sealed and hung carefully on rubber shock cords in the cockpit. After use, it is calibrated by the United States Bureau of Standards—that is, the actual height attained is determined.

For this official test, besides the barograph, I took along a bottle of oxygen. Beyond sixteen thousand feet it is well to have some on tap if a pilot intends to stay aloft a long time or to go higher. As it turned out, I reached only 18,415 feet and my lungs seemed to do the job unassisted.

Colonel and Mrs. Charles A. Lindbergh

Three stages of a parachute jump

I suppose the temperature was about zero at that height, but my heavy flying suit, boots and mittens kept me comfortable.

The higher one goes on a clear day, the more of the world one can see. Distances shrink and cities and town miles apart look as if they were neighboring stops on the Toonerville Trolley line. Possibly in the future, sightseeing tours may be arranged to take passengers not only from place to place but to different "levels."

SEE THE NATION'S CAPITOL
(and 25 surrounding towns)
From 10,000 feet   For 25c.

SEE THE NATION'S CAPITOL
(and 100 surrounding towns)
From 20,000 feet   For 50c.

Well, I hope the passengers will enjoy the scenery as much as I do when I fly high.

Not long after the altitude hop, I started across the country in an autogiro. I went definitely on a commercial venture, for I carried a large sign on the fuselage for the *Beech-Nut Packing Company*. Up to the present writing the most practical use to which 'giros have been put is advertising various products. Everything from coal to gasoline has been sold in this manner. Getting a trade mark before large numbers of people has been done as effectively by means of flying signboards as by those which stay on the ground.

But my personal reasons for making this trip was to test the autogiro on a long trip, under all kinds of weather conditions. I wished to know for myself just what it could do and what its future possibilities might reasonably be.

I made the journey to the coast via the northern mail route where no autogiros had ever been before. When I landed at Oakland, California, mine was the second to reach the west. I started back from Los Angeles, but alas, did not arrive intact. Texas proved my Waterloo for I had an accident there that considerably damaged the faithful ship.

As luck would have it, I had an engagement to appear with it two days later in a middle western city. By unmercifully lashing another 'giro and using his spurs, an accommodating pilot managed to arrive from Philadelphia just in time for me to go on with the scheduled performance. Afterward I went east with the second 'giro, while the pilot saw that my wreck was crated and sent to the factory for repairs.

While I regret any kind of accident, I have found they are sometimes of benefit. So it was in this particular case. I learned a great deal—all of it valuable experience with this new kind of plane.

Speaking of plane accidents in general, I might add that women are often penalized by publicity for their every mishap. Any disproportionate "breaks" they get when they accomplish something are nullified in crash headlines. Probably the most unfortunate result is that such emphasis sometimes directly affects chances for flying jobs. I had one manufacturer tell me that he couldn't risk hiring women pilots because of the way accidents, even minor ones, were played up in the newspapers.

"A man can damage a plane and hardly a word be said," he explained, "but that doesn't apply when sister stubs her toe. I don't want my products advertised by a nose-over or a forced landing. But don't misunderstand me," he hastened to add. "I don't mean women have more accidents than men."

With flippant inaccuracy the magazine *Time* referred to my Texas episode under the caption (as I remember it) "First Autogiro Crackup."

And so it goes.

There is another point to be mentioned in connection with women and accidents. That is, everyone should realize there will be an inevitable increase in the number of casualties involving women. I do not mean the *proportion* of accidents to the number of pilots will increase, but only that as more and more women enter into aviation, the number of accidents may be expected to keep pace.

What the comparative accident rate between feminine and masculine pilots is, or will be, I do not know. There are some reasons for saying that women for a time, owing to lack of experience, may have more. A likely example of why I say so is afforded in certain changes in flying conditions today from a few years ago. When some of the veteran men pilots learned to fly there were very few kinds of planes available. Further, they were all slow and with motors of limited horsepower. As the planes were improved and speeded up, the pilots progressed gradually from one type to another, learning each.

Now the picture is quite altered. Anyone who has the money can buy a tricky racing plane if desired, and fly (or try to fly) it. The long enforced process of gaining experience is gone, and only common sense, when it exists, remains as a safeguard. Without the background of knowing the full value of experience, I sometimes think women are more apt to attempt a bigger bite than they can successfully chew than are men. (This may apply in more quarters than in aviation.)

In other words, what has happened with automobiles will inevitably happen with airplanes. More cars on the road have meant more accidents—but not necessarily *in proportion.* More women drivers has brought about more accidents with women drivers—but not necessarily *in proportion.*

One more thought. A fatal accident to a woman pilot is not a greater disaster than one to a man of equal worth. Feminine flyers have never subscribed to the super-sentimental valuation placed upon their necks. I am sure they feel they can endure their share of misfortune, whatever it be, as quietly as men.

There are still some more things I want to say

about autogiros. I am often asked whether other kinds can be built. The answer is yes—big transports are possible, and little fast single seaters. The theory is good for all.

It seems to me whether or not the autogiro ever invades the general field of aeronautical activity that one of its accomplishments—that of hovering in the air under certain conditions—will be utilized for special work. Perhaps it will be found especially adaptable in aerial photography. There are surely scores of special uses to which it might attain. In fact, with the giro as with many new developments, so much is likely to happen that I am planning to return to earth in a couple of hundred years to check up on its doings.

WOMEN AND AVIATION

A T a woman's club not long ago I was asked to talk about opportunities for women in commercial aviation. When I had finished painting the picture as best I could, the chairman remarked,

"Well, you certainly spoiled all my illusions. I thought girls could get any jobs they wanted in aviation by just asking for them."

In any discussion of the subject one must first separate actual flying and some special positions from all other types of employment in aviation. Also it will be necessary to explain that "aviation" includes aircraft divisions of various allied industries—such as precision instruments manufacture, for instance. Even with these widened boundaries the number of women employed in all is very small. Their proportion to men as given by a Labor Bureau survey is about one to forty-four. Some concerns do not employ women at all, and in those which do, they are often paid only about half as much as men.

Most of the feminine labor is used in the wing departments for sewing the fabric used in wing covering. There are, however, several women welders and some inspectors in engine planes. The Naval Aircraft Factory in Philadelphia lists several women employees, and in the building of the dirigibles, the *Shenandoah* and the *Akron,* women were employed in the construction of the gas cells and in the application of gold beater's skin to them. There are a few one-of-a-kind factory jobs, existing perhaps because of an individual's unusual ability and because such a worker doesn't interfere much with men's employment.

As I have indicated before, the aircraft divisions of rubber, petroleum and instrument companies, to mention only a few of the ramifications of the industry, utilize women in various capacities. Closely allied to aviation as a useful parasite, is the manufacturing of parachutes. There women almost exclusively cut and sew the fabric but men pack the finished products into covers.

Aside from factory work, there is clerical help to be considered. As in all industries, much of it is now designated definitely as "women's work", and so wherever filing, stenography, and similar tasks are necessary, women are found. The offices where they work are not always in town. Often they are on or adjacent to an airport or testing field where the staff can see something of actual flying activities.

Many people think of aviation as composed almost entirely of pilots. They overlook the great non-flying group of workers who are necessary to build the planes, and keep them running. With increasing air travel on the part of the public, an army of traffic men, ticket sellers, accountants, and mechanics, all under trained heads, *besides* pilots, are needed to operate the country's great network of airlines. In this group as well as in factories and executive offices, women play their part, but their part is almost without exception in the clerical end.

If I were to count only pilots, there would be not one woman discovered in the cockpit of any scheduled airplane. (By scheduled I mean time-table operated, i.e. the regular service of aircraft leaving a port at a given time to arrive at another similarly.) However, there are women who do earn their living by flying. They sell airplanes, they ferry planes about the country, they carry passengers, they instruct, they fly in the promotion department of a few companies who use airplanes for advertising and for transporting their executives.

As to special positions, there are a number worthy of mention. Several women own or manage airports; several conduct schools, alone or with their husbands; several hold traffic positions of varying importance; one designs the interiors of passenger airliners. There are two women examiners in the medical staff of the Aeronautics Branch, Department of Commerce. A number of women are associated with the journals of the trade. One conducts a special page, another is assistant editor, others write articles for use inside and outside this special field. There are one or two women publicity writers and of course many touch aviation through advertising. One of the most able and accurate artists on aircraft drawing for advertising (or any other work for that matter) is a woman. Two airlines employ women as hostesses on their

large cabin planes. Everyone is familiar with the
number of women who manage travel bureaus
throughout the country. Most of these handle airline tickets now, and there is one with a feminine
owner which caters only to air travelers.

Despite the number and variety of those positions, it must be admitted there is definite prejudice
against women in certain departments. Possibly it
is no greater than in other industries. At any rate,
I shall not attempt to go into details concerning it
except in regard to actual flying. There I think
some explanation might be of interest, as training,
practise and tradition are involved.

Since the early days of flying not many women
have received as adequate training as men. The
best schools in many ways at least, are the Army
and Navy, and they, of course, are closed to women.
Commercial institutions until recently apparently
did not particularly welcome feminine students and
had little conscience about their adequate instruction.

It has always seemed to me that boys and girls
are educated very differently. Even from the early
grades, they take different subjects. For instance,
boys are usually put into woodworking classes, and
girls into sewing or cooking—willy-nilly. I know
many boys who should, I am sure, be making pies
and girls who are much better fitted for manual
training than domestic science. Too often little attention is paid to individual talent. Instead, education goes on dividing people according to their

sex, and putting them in little feminine or masculine pigeonholes.

Outside of school, similar differences are noticeable, too. In the home, boys and girls usually follow the pursuits which tradition has decreed for the one and the other. As different as what they do are ways of doing it. Girls are shielded and sometimes helped so much that they lose initiative and begin to believe the signs "Girls don't" and "Girls can't" which mark their paths. Mrs. Bertrand Russell puts this fact very forcibly when she says women are bred to timidity.

It is not surprising then that as boys and girls grow older their backgrounds become more and more unlike. Consequently, it seems almost necessary to evolve different methods of instruction for them when they later take up the same subjects. For example, those courses which involve mechanical work may have to be explained somewhat differently to girls not because girls are *inherently* not mechanical, but because normally they have learned little about such things in the course of their education.

I could illustrate this idea the other way around. I once watched the progress of a boys' cooking class. The teacher started out with the same method of approach as she used for the girls. What happened? Her pupils were so stupid she was almost ready to believe the masculine mind incapable of comprehending the rudiments of boiling eggs. However, being a resourceful instructor, it didn't take her long to find out what was wrong. *Of course* boys didn't know dishwater should be soapy. Of course they didn't know ovens should be hot for biscuit, and of course they didn't know a dozen other fundamentals that girls picked up before they ever came to class.

So—by including some explanations unnecessary for girls in the general method, pie-making went on apace. In the same way, feminine students in flying schools might gain more if courses were modified or adjusted to their educational needs.

Just as there may be some handicaps in training, so there may be in finances. Most girls are not able to earn as much as boys, particularly around airports, yet they must pay the same price for flying lessons. No one wants a feminine "grease monkey" around the hangar to do the odd jobs which may partly pay for a young man's aviation training. Then, too, with fewer outlets to earn money after they have their flying license, they must hesitate longer about deciding on an aviation career.

There are also minor hindrances in the construction of airplanes. Such things as brakes and starters are sometimes so obviously designed or located for masculine hands or feet that small women pilots have discomfort if not difficulty in using them. Some of the smallest women have to stuff pillows around them to make the cockpit fit.

Probably the most profound deterrent of all is tradition which keeps women from trying new things and from putting forth their whole effort

when once they do venture forth. It also makes
men unwilling to recognize women's abilities. Consequently they sometimes feel that they must do
foolhardy or silly things just to prove they can.

There are 472 licensed women pilots in the
United States. Of these about fifty hold the transport or highest grade. 472 seems a large number
when it is remembered there were but twelve
women licensees in January, 1929. However, it
shrinks to a proportion of about 1 to 37 in the face
of the entire pilots listing (men and women) which
is 17,226 strong (October, 1931). Taking into
consideration only the 50 transport licenses, for
none other can really be counted as offering commercial possibilities, the number of potential candidates among women for available jobs, if any, is
exceedingly small.

Despite these figures, there are more women
flyers in the United States than in all the rest of
the world, and it follows more in commercial aviation. Further, it appears they do more together
in this country than anywhere else. They not only
compete in exclusive racing events, but have recently conducted several entire air meets by themselves. Besides organizations composed of women
interested in aviation generally, there are some for
women pilots only. Oldest among these is the
Ninety-Nines, open to any woman holding a current Department of Commerce license. Another
is the *Betsy Ross Corps,* established to train picked

women for service to their country in time of need.
The Women's Air Reserve of California is another
specialized group.

Among non-professional clubs is the Women's
National Aeronautic Association, with chapters in
nearly every state. This group has done especially
appreciated work in providing comfortable quarters at many airports for other women who arrive
by air.

Because there are still comparatively few of
these, facilities for feminine comfort are all too
often overlooked at flying fields. To me, it is sometimes worth going a hundred miles out of the way
to land at ports like Akron, Ohio, where the
Women's Aeronautic Association has furnished a
pilot's lounge complete with everything from powder puffs to showers. Usually when pilots and
passengers are so well treated, motors and airplanes
can find adequate care, also.

In any discussion of women and aviation, the
means by which some of the pilots have earned their
licenses should be included.

Many and varied these have been. Perhaps more
have labored within the ranks of the industry than
outside, for sometimes a connection, even on the
fringe, has made possible special encouragement in
the way of rates or use of equipment. Often just
being with a group who doesn't think flying
strange, is a help in itself. Jean La Rene of
Dallas, one of the best known southern fliers, dem-

onstrates this theory for she is secretary for an aviation school, and gets in considerable flying by just being on hand.

As to those who earn money for their flying in totally different fields, their occupations range all the way from selling real estate to acting. The names of several school teachers now appear on the pilot's list and bookkeepers and stenographers, too. One girl I know of waited on table in a restaurant to gain her license, and another won a scholarship to a private pilot's rating. Still another sold the idea to business men of her home town that they should underwrite her training. More than one newspaper woman has used her writing ability to pay for a course of instruction.

As well known as any of this plucky band is Viola Gentry. She was a cashier in a Brooklyn cafeteria and saved enough to get a license. After this she toiled to promote and prepare a refueling flight with another pilot. Through no fault of hers the plane cracked up and she was painfully injured. It has taken her many long months to recover sufficiently to return to her job, and it will be longer still before she can regain her license.

Bobby Trout, co-holder of the women's refueling record, is another pilot who has worked hard for what she has accomplished. She owns and operates a service station in California.

Now and then, girls marry into flying and become wives of men who can and do teach them. That is one way to get the coveted lessons, but probably not advisable unless the gentlemen in question possess other charms in addition to being good instructors.

By the way, I have not yet heard of a wife teaching her *husband* to fly, but Mary Alexander of Lynchburg, Virginia, should qualify for the next award as she has a nineteen-year-old son whom she has instructed. She is famous too for being a very young flying grandmother, for her son himself is the proud father of an infant. Mrs. Mary Bain, wife of a mining engineer, is the other flying grandmother I mentioned.

Some of those who haven't actually held positions, yet belong to the determined-to-fly group, are women who have saved their money from allowances or household expenses. I know one girl who spends most of what her father gives her for clothes, on flying. He loves to have her well dressed, but has just about given up hope of seeing her in anything other than monkey suits.

While it may be difficult enough to learn to fly if one does not have an airminded Santa Claus in the family, often the hardest part is keeping on flying after the instruction period is over. Renting equipment is expensive and many a long day goes by before an employer can be persuaded to risk his airplane on a novice pilot's skill—much less pay him to fly. You wouldn't lend your nice new shiny automobile to someone who had just learned to drive, or hire a chauffeur who didn't have a record of long experience. Neither should I, and the aircraft owner, airline operator or manufacturer, feels about a hundred times as strongly as we do.

However, one girl who has made good almost from the start is Dorothy Hester. She was taught to stunt by Tex Rankin of Portland and found to be an apt pupil. She and her instructor now give exhibitions at meets and she is developing into an excellent performer.

Those who have worked for their flying are not the only ones, by any means, who have put energy and skill into it. Some of the best pilots among women are non-professionals of whom Betty Huyler Gillies of New York is an excellent example. Her husband is chief engineer in an aircraft factory and an ex-navy flier and both he and she have planes.

Maude Tait, winner of the Aerol Trophy race in 1931, is a newcomer among pilots, but certainly a skilled one. A "borderline" case is Florence (Pancho) Barnes of California. She qualifies as a sportsman pilot, I am sure, but now and then also accepts special commissions. For instance, she did some of the flying in the motion picture, "Hell's Angels."

With these brief histories of a few of today's women fliers, it looks as if nearly everyone who really wants to fly somehow manages it despite obstacles. Perhaps what is necessary for success is a large quantity of the same kind of enthusiasm which actuates a young flying couple I met recently. The feminine partner confided to me her

Ruth Law greeted by General Leonard Wood on her
arrival at Governor's Island

Katherine Stinson

family objected strenuously to her flying because they thought she couldn't earn her living by it.

"Well," she said as she glanced at a big cabin plane nearby, "when my husband and I started out we had nothing—nothing at all. Now we have this ship to use for instruction and charter trips."

"We'll take anybody anywhere anytime," her husband spoke up.

"What fun you must have adventuring together," I said.

"Well, we do—most of the time," she answered. "Of course, now and then it's hard to get along. But I'd rather be poor and fly than have more and do something else."

WE TAKE TO THE AIR

THE event which started concerted activity among women fliers was the cross country air derby for women of 1929. This was a race which started on the West Coast and ended eight days later at Cleveland, Ohio.

Sunday afternoon August 18, nineteen planes with propellers turning, lined up at Clover Field, Santa Monica, California. Will Rogers was on the loud speaker to point out the humorous aspects of such an event. Taking their cue from him, newspaper men coined descriptive names for the affair before contestants reached their first stop. It was generally called the "powder puff derby" and those who flew in it variously as "Ladybirds", "Angels" or "Sweethearts of the Air". (We are still trying to get ourselves called just "pilots".)

Finishing a race, as in anything else, is as important as starting, and sixteen of the women crossed the white line at the end. This was the highest per cent of "finishers" in any cross country derby, up to that time, for men or women.

This first air derby was won by Louise Thaden of Pittsburgh, with Gladys O'Donnell of California, second and me third. It captured the public interest and proved invaluable in interesting other women in aviation. A large part of the crowds which greeted the derby at the prearranged stops along the route were women. They came to see what the powder puffers themselves looked like and after that what kind of airplanes they had. Some were so interested in these they poked umbrellas through the fabric on the wings to discover what was inside. Since then I have maintained that women's hesitancy in accepting air travel is simply because they are uninformed about it. What people don't understand, they usually fear.

Funny and serious situations continuously arose behind the scenes on the race. Blanche Noyes discovered fire in the baggage compartment of her plane and had to come down on a mesquite covered section of western Texas to put it out. No one knows how she managed to land without damaging the plane nor how she took off again from such a place.

Now and then some of the inexperienced pilots got lost, some ran out of gasoline, some were forced down by motor trouble. During the course of the race, more than one had to pick out the best spot available and make an unscheduled descent. Of course, when a pilot finds it necessary to land away from an established airport he—or she—heads for a good big pasture if one is around. One day one of the girls had to seek a pasture for some reason and the best one she saw had animals in it. Nevertheless she landed safely and then to her consternation watched the creatures solemnly walk toward her. Her version of the story is that she promptly offered up a little prayer. It was "Dear God, let them all be cows."

Speaking of cows, I am reminded of one of the most famous of air mail stories. Dean Smith flew the route from New York to Cleveland for a good many years. On one occasion, when his motor failed him, he too sought a pasture for a landing. Unfortunately, the "animals" in it were not well behaved for they stood in his way and he landed directly on one. The following is in substance the account of the accident which he telegraphed to his chief—

"Motor cut. Forced landing. Hit cow. Cow died. Scared me."

To return to the derby, it is but fair to give credit where it is due. The race was arranged and its prizes financed by the National Exchange Clubs, an organization which I believe has done more to aid aviation than any other non-professional group in America.

It is interesting to compare the status of women flying in 1929 with their position today. To be eligible for the 1929 derby, a current license and a minimum of one hundred hours' solo flying were required. I doubt whether more than thirty American women could have qualified. But of this possible thirty, twenty turned out.

In 1929, only seven women held Department of Commerce Transport licenses and six of these were in the race. Today, as I have said before, there are more than seven times this number. In addi-

tion to these and the 450 LC's and Privates,
twelve women hold glider licenses and five are licensed mechanics.

Although only two years separates them, it is a
far cry from the pioneering derby performance to
women's share in the National Air Races in Cleveland in 1931. There for the first time in the United
States men and women participated in a cross country derby together. There were about fifty en-
trants whose planes had been handicapped on the
basis of their top speeds.

Unlike the British, the Americans have done
little mixed racing, nor have they favored any system of handicapping. The method of determining
classes has been almost universally based on size of
motors. Thus, a cabin airplane built to carry six
passengers might be placed in the same class with a
strictly racing plane carrying only the pilot because
both had engines with the same cubic inch displace-
ment.

In England, on the other hand, almost all racing
has been carried on with the fast planes starting
late to give the slower ones a chance—motors not
being considered. So that, barring an accident,
good piloting wins or loses. The King's Cup Race,
the most famous annual cross country event, is run
in this manner, and is open to all pilots of both
sexes. Miss Winifred Brown is the only woman
who has won it (1930).

While the 1931 American derby pilots raced over
the same course, made the same stops, and were

judged by the same officials, there were separate prizes in the men's classification and so, also, for the women. However, a sweepstakes was offered to the winner, irrespective of sex, who had the highest total of points. This prize, $2500.00, and a new automobile was won by a woman, Phoebe Omlie, of Memphis, Tennessee. Mrs. Omlie, by the way, won several thousand dollars in addition to this in the closed course races, and was one of the heaviest winners among competing women pilots. Among other prize winners were May Haizlip, Maude Tait, Gladys O'Donnell and Florence Klingensmith.

One of the best races for men is the justly famous Thompson Trophy event. It is to land planes what the Schneider Cup has been to seaplanes. In other words it is the aerial speed classic of the year.

Corresponding to this is the Aerol Trophy Race for women for maximum speed over a closed course. In 1931 the distance was fifty miles, made in five laps of a ten-mile course, the flyer rounding four markers. The home pylon, as the markers are called, is directly in front of the grandstand, while the other three simply define the boundaries of the course to be flown.

The highest speed made in this race was 187 miles an hour, attained by Maude Tait in her Gee Bee sport plane. This time, it is interesting to notice, is less than fifteen miles slower than that of the best record made by men in the Thompson Trophy race of the year before—which goes to show that selected women flyers, if given opportunity and equipment, may be expected to tread pretty closely upon the heels of their male competitors.

In the 1931 National Air Races, men and women had separate events as usual. However, during the year, throughout the country there were an increasing number of contests in which both sexes participated, solely as pilots. Slowly the prejudice against women is lessening, and it appears probable that before long they will compete in major speed events on equal terms.

Whatever handicaps in tradition, training or experience women face they do not have to overcome any as far as Department of Commerce licenses are concerned. In this connection, they are more fortunate than some of their sisters abroad. Some countries issue only restricted licenses to women and in some, women cannot hold any, so far as I can find out. England is the notable exception and follows the same rule as does the United States, i.e., if a candidate passes physical and flying tests a license is issued according to qualifications irrespective of sex.

The Fédération Aéronautique Internationale governs the aeronautical sporting events here and abroad, and is in charge of all record flights. The National Aeronautic Association is the representative in the United States of that body. No pilot can make an official test for altitude, speed or distance without its sanction. Its representatives are on hand to supervise all efforts at record making.

Since the establishment of the F. A. I. twenty-

five years ago, there had been only one category for
aeronautical attainments. No one could have fore-
seen what limits of speed or endurance or altitude
airplanes would reach. In 1905 there were so few
pilots, that classifying them would have been a joke.
During the war, however, the number of pilots and
airplanes increased tremendously and records
thought impossible once, began to be made. But
women didn't really become very active until 1929,
as I have described previously. Certainly they had
not progressed to the point where they figured in
any of the records made. They had neither the
experience nor the equipment to attain world recognition in any of the classifications. Consequently, any efforts they made were labeled unoffi-
cial despite the fact they were as carefully judged
and tabulated as were those which men were continuously writing in the annals of the F. A. I.

"Why," asked Mr. General Public, "is Mary
Smith's altitude record of umpty-ump thousand
feet not official? That's higher than any other
woman has flown, isn't it?"

"Yes," was the answer, "but it isn't higher than
men have gone. As there are not separate records
for women, the only ones which are official must exceed theirs."

After earnest requests from various women fliers
separate classifications were set up. Thus, they can
fly as high and as fast and as far as they are able,
and if they exceed what other women have done,
they may earn official recognition. If they exceed

the marks made by any other flyer whomsoever, they may hold title to world records.

While no woman at present holds a world record, Maryse Bastie of France has been officially credited with staying aloft for thirty-seven hours and fifty-five minutes consecutively—longer than anyone else has ever done alone. She does not rate a world record, however, as a solo performance is not differentiated from that where two or more pilots are together and can "spell" each other. As a matter of fact, the United States holds this particular International one with eighty-four hours and thirty-two minutes.

Perhaps I should explain what world records are. There are only five of them and they are—greatest altitude, maximum speed over a three kilometer straightaway course, greatest distance measured in a straight line, endurance flying around a closed circuit, and endurance flying just staying aloft and landing at the place of take off.

In other words the most successful performance in any of these fields rates as a world record, no matter who makes it nor what type of aircraft he or she uses. However, there are many, many other official records besides these to be tried for. They are in a group classified not as World but as International and are subdivided into many categories. Thus there are altitude and speed records for small land planes, for example, and similar ones for large models. Speed runs may be made empty or with specified loads over specified distances, depending on just which record the pilot aims to establish. Thus, on the list of women record holders, May Haizlip is credited with an altitude record of 18,097 feet in a light airplane. That means she has gone higher in that class (18,097 feet) than any other woman and so holds the international record. Of course, it wouldn't be fair to compare what her little Bull Pup can do with what a plane with a motor twice as powerful could accomplish—which is an illustration of the reason for the subdivisions.

INTERNATIONAL FEMININE RECORDS

LANDPLANES

Duration (France) Maryse Bastie, 37 hours 55 minutes:
  Klemm airplane, Salmson 40 h.p. engine
  Le Bourget, September 2, 3, 4, 1930
Altitude (United States) Ruth Nichols, 28,743 feet:
  Lockheed Vega monoplane, Pratt and Whitney Wasp
  420 h.p.
  Jersey City Airport, New Jersey, March 6, 1931
Maximum speed (U. S.) Ruth Nichols, 210.63 miles per
  hour:
  Lockheed Vega monoplane, P and W "Wasp" 420 h.p.
  Carleton, Michigan, April 13, 1931
Distance—airline (U. S.)—Ruth Nichols, 1977.6 miles:
  Lockheed Vega monoplane
Speed for 100 kilometers (U. S.) Amelia Earhart, 174.89
  mph:
  Lockheed Vega monoplane, P and W Wasp, 420 h.p.
  Detroit, Michigan, June 25, 1930.

Speed for 100 kilometers with payload of 500 kilograms
(U. S.) :
Amelia Earhart, 171.43 miles per hour
Lockheed Vega monoplane, P and W Wasp, 420 h.p.
Detroit, Michigan, June 25, 1930
Duration with refueling in flight (United States) :
Evelyn Trout and Edna May Cooper, 123 hours
Curtiss Robin monoplane, Challenger 170 h.p. engine
Los Angeles, California, January 4–9, 1931

LIGHT AIRPLANES

Distance airline (France) Maryse Bastie, 1849.76 miles :
Klemm airplane, Salmson 40 h.p. engine
Le Bourget, France, to Urino, Russia, June 28–30,
1930
Altitude (United States) May Haizlip, 18,097 feet
Buhl "Bull Pup," Szekeley 85 h.p. engine
St. Clair, Michigan, June 13, 1931

SEAPLANES

Altitude (United States) Marion Eddy Conrad, 13,461.25
feet
Savoia-Marchetti airplane, Kinner 125 h.p. engine
Port Washington, Long Island, October 20, 1930

Records as such may or may not be important,
but at least the more of them women make, the
more forcefully is it demonstrated that they can
and do fly. Directly or indirectly, more opportunities for those who wish to enter the aviation world
should be opened by such evidence.

During the last few years a dozen or more American women have been doing progressively fine flying. Much of it has been true pioneering, for a number of those who are most active are really professionals and make their living from aviation.

What are women flyers like? What do they do when not flying? How do they look? These questions are still asked so often that I am going to describe a few of those I know.

Of course, they are not different as individuals from any other group. There are slim ones and plump ones and quiet ones and those who talk all the time. They're large and small, young and old, about half the list are married and many of these have children. In a word, they are simply thoroughly normal girls and women who happen to have taken up flying rather than golf, swimming or steeplechasing.

Ruth Nichols is one of the most active record holders among women flyers, yet flying does not fill her time by any means. She lives at Rye, New York, not far from my own home, so I see her driving her car, swimming, riding, and doing just about everything you would expect a modern young woman to do outdoors as well as in. She is a graduate of Wellesley College and during her college career majored in Bible History and Literature. In her third year there she approached the dean with the idea of flying.

"Miss Blank, I think I should like to learn to fly."

"Fly?" queried the dean. "My dear young lady, I have enough to do with several hundred students as it is. Motor cars brought trouble of their own. Now I certainly am not going to add any more by admitting airplanes, too. No, you may not fly."

Despite her arguments, she could not change that decree. So Ruth abandoned Wellesley for one year and took her flying lessons off campus. Her instructor was Harry Rodgers and in a short time he soloed her on seaplanes at Port Washington, Long Island. Later, with Captain Rodgers, she made the first non-stop flight from New York to Miami in twelve hours.

After graduation—she returned to college to get her degree—she became assistant to the head of the woman's department of the National City Bank of New York. This was the beginning of her business career. She subsequently became the first woman director of a large aviation corporation.

In 1928 Miss Nichols had an important part in the organization of Aviation Country Clubs, formed by a group of sportsmen pilots who wanted the advantages of a country club with flying added. The first of these clubs was opened at Hicksville, Long Island. In their interest Ruth made a 12,000 mile solo flight with an escorting plane. On this long journey she landed in 96 cities and 48 states without a forced landing.

She was one of the competitors in the famous 1929 transcontinental derby. And since then she has done her share of distinguished flying. In solo

flight, she has been to date officially higher, faster
and farther in a straight line than any other woman.
On March 6, 1931, she attained an altitude of
27,740 feet, besting the record previously held by
Elinor Smith. In April of 1931, in her Wasp
powered Lockheed, she established a speed record
at Carleton, Michigan, attaining 210 miles per
hour. In this, she excelled the record of 181 miles
per hour I had set the year before. Then in October,
1931, on an attempted non-stop flight from California to New York, she established a new long distance record for women. She landed in Louisville,
Kentucky, after covering 1977 miles without a stop
—568 miles farther than Maryse Bastie of France
had flown.

Miss Nichols has also to her credit an east-west
transcontinental record of sixteen hours, fifty-nine
and one-half minutes and a women's west-east
transcontinental record of thirteen hours twenty-
one minutes. Both of these, of course, are reckoned
on actual flying time and not elapsed time. That
is, when she stopped for motor check and to refuel
and over night at Wichita, time was taken out. Up
to now, no women have made non stop transcontinental hops. But perhaps by the time you read
this that statement may not be true.

Miss Nichols' flying advisor is Clarence Chamberlin, the famous pilot who took Levine across the
Atlantic in 1927. It is he who helped her in her
plans for a solo transatlantic flight. While the
first plane she obtained for this was damaged in a

small field at St. John, New Brunswick, I suspect it is only a matter of time before she tries again.

I think Miss Nichols is probably the only woman in captivity who has delivered by plane one brother to an army air training station. Recently, she ferried the elder of her two younger brothers to Kelly Field where he is completing his training. By the way, the other one is working at one of the Long Island airports and is earning his license there. Her sister is secretary for a flyer, and that puts the whole family into aviation as far as the younger generation goes. The others only ride.

Ruth Nichols always dresses with charm and distinction. Even in the air she is apt to be garbed in her favorite color, which happens to be purple, and she owns a specially made purple leather flying suit and helmet.

Another well known flyer is Elinor Smith. Before Miss Nichols captured it, she held the altitude record for women with a mark of 27,418 feet. After it was taken from her, she promptly went up to get it back. In this attempt she fainted at 25,000 feet, when her oxygen tube broke, and fell four miles through the air before she regained consciousness. She was only two thousand feet above the earth at that moment, yet managed to get control of her plane and land in a vacant lot. Then, just to show she hadn't lost her nerve, she tried again for the altitude record the following week.

It has been said of Miss Smith that she learned to fly almost as soon as she learned to walk. Be that as it may, she made her first official flight, at least, at the age of eight. In those days the Smith family lived near the old Curtiss Field on Long Island and Elinor's father, who is an actor, found himself succumbing to the lure of flying. Elinor, then about ten, used to play around while her father took instruction. Various pilots were forever taking her up and letting her handle the controls in the air.

I believe she was fifteen when her father bought a plane, and it was hard for her to learn that she could not solo until she was eighteen. It appears that she couldn't wait, for she arranged for some lessons with a little money of her own. Every morning she arose at five and sneaked away for her instruction, returning home to be "waked" for school. By the time her parents discovered what she was up to, she really felt herself a pretty good pilot.

Elinor Smith commenced making her mark in flying when she was only eighteen. In October, 1928, she attracted plenty of attention—and trouble for herself—by flying under all the East River bridges one Sunday afternoon. This prank caused the Department of Commerce to suspend her license temporarily. Three months later, she went up after the solo endurance record for women held by Bobby Trout. It was the end of January and for thirteen hours in an open cockpit plane she circled the Long Island flying fields. Then, the story goes, she saw lights flashing from

Ruth Nichols

Luftfahrt der Mad Reichardt auf der Theresien Wiese am Oktober Feste zu München 1820.

Ballooning in Germany

the ground which she thought were signals that
something was wrong. So she landed, half frozen
—only to find out that she was an hour—but only
an hour—on the long side of the previous record.
Then Bobby Trout took the record back and after
that Louise Thaden had it for a while, until Elinor
Smith went up again and stayed for twenty-six
hours or more. In this country that mark still
stands.

In 1929 she and Bobby Trout tried a refueling
flight in California. In a ship that was not really
fit for the job, they contrived to stay aloft forty-two
hours. They only came down then because their
refueling partners had motor trouble and couldn't
service them longer.

Miss Smith has flown many kinds of planes and
flown them well. She likes to fly big ones, and I
think she has a real philosophy for doing so. At
least, she is quoted as having said, "If you come in
with a light plane, nobody pays any attention to
you. Heavy planes aren't really any harder to
handle, but people think they are. They think
women can only handle little ones." In which there
is a great deal of truth.

In flying, as in many modern pursuits, a certain
amount of showmanship helps one to get over the
rough spots—especially if flying is a profession and
competition hard.

Among the jobs connected with aviation which
Miss Smith has developed is broadcasting a weekly
aviation news radio talk. She has also proved very

successful as radio announcer at air meets, for she speaks fluently, has real wit, and knows nearly everyone in the field.

Miss Smith's clothes can usually be counted on for a surprise. She is apt to wear whatever fancy or comfort of the moment dictates. At air meets I have seen her in costumes that range from conventional riding breeches to bright red beach overalls or shorts.

Verily, clothes don't make a pilot, and pilots, men or women, may wear almost any kind they choose and still fly.

I think I should pause and emphasize this point a bit. Since the public has only recently learned that flying is not a thing totally apart from other human activities, only recently have pilots been able to fly in everyday clothes. At one time unless they dressed as "aviators," they were likely to be regarded with suspicion. To do my part in making aviation appear as normal as possible, I decided several years ago to abandon special togs and to wear only conventional sport clothes, with skirts, around airports and while flying. Sometimes I even omitted a helmet and pulled on my goggles over a close fitting hat. Thus I entered my plane as matter-of-factly as I did a car—and nearly always surprised onlookers thereby.

Those days are over. The increasing familiarity of people with cabin planes and aviation in general has lightened this and other loads which devotees such as I assumed for the good of the cause. We can now wear nearly anything we choose with practicality—and sometimes price—the deciding factors. Of course an exception is the case of airline pilots who must wear uniforms while on duty. Then, too, there is one of the women pilots who insists she doesn't get service at airports if she wears street clothing even though she arrives in a closed plane where there is no necessity for trousers of any sort. When she does venture forth in skirts, she keeps a helmet on the seat beside her to clap on her head after landing to impress attendants.

So clothes have an important relation to aviation. I have mentioned them throughout this book because I think they not only may characterize individuals but throw a side light on the development of the industry as a whole.

To return to Elinor Smith, these days she has a fast Lockheed, such as Miss Nichols has used, and no one knows what is up her sleeve.

SOME FEMININE FLYERS

PERHAPS no woman flyer is more interesting than Anne Lindbergh. That is because of her own personality, the fame of her husband, and the way in which she has tackled flying.

Anne Lindbergh is an extremely gentle person, essentially modest, totally lacking mannerisms, pretenses and superiorities. She is small, yet she has a charming dignity when surrounded by people. Most notable of her physical features are her large blue eyes which look out from long lashes, often with a quizzical gleam, directly and frankly at everyone—except perhaps news photographers! Her bobbed brown hair is combed back in a natural wave from a wide intelligent forehead. Her skin is fair and clear. About her mouth a smile always seems to lurk.

Her dress is simple, like her direct manners. As pilot or passenger, she shuns affectations. Ordinary street or sport clothes suffice, except when she plans to fly in an open cockpit where cold makes flying suits more comfortable. Then, her diminutive figure engulfed in ungainly togs, she looks like a tiny teddy bear beside her six-foot-something husband.

Mrs. Lindbergh, who first soloed at the Aviation Country Club at Hicksville, Long Island, obtained her private license in 1931.

"What kind of individual is Mrs. Lindbergh,

anyway?" a reporter asked me. "What does she do? What does she say? You know to the world she is a woman of mystery."

Under the circumstances I could tell him nothing. But there are no secrets about her—just natural reticences. Mrs. Lindbergh is an unusual person but not mysterious. She does what she wishes. She reads, writes, and drives her own car. She slips out of the house when she pleases and goes where she pleases. I do not know what games, if any, she likes or what sports.

"Do you really like to fly?"

"What actually are the sensations of flying?"

Those two questions are most often asked Mrs. Lindbergh—mostly by other women. That second query, of course, is asked of all who are associated with aviation in any capacity. As to the first, I think it will surprise many to know that even before she met Colonel Lindbergh, Anne Morrow was enough interested in flying to have decided she would herself learn to handle an airplane sometime.

Mrs. Lindbergh once said substantially this to me in California. She was quiet, sincere, simply making a statement to another woman who, like herself, travels mostly by air. In speaking of her own flying, she was careful to make her attitude clear. It was not to be her business, but she felt that any woman who took it up professionally could find in it the greatest interest and enjoyment.

She went on to outline what one might call "the philosophy of flying" of one who is undoubtedly today America's best-known woman—flyer and flyee combined. It is simply this, that aviation is one of the most progress-bringing occupations today. It is a new kind of transportation, and as such, is an important part of living. It does not lie so close to humanity's primal needs as food-getting or shelter requirements, but it means a great deal in satisfaction and comfort and in the distribution of much that is desirable.

I first met Mrs. Lindbergh at the opening of the forty-eight-hour coast-to-coast service inaugurated by Transcontinental Air Transport when I was one of the passengers on the first-west-bound plane. Colonel Lindbergh brought the first one eastward from Los Angeles, and in Arizona changed to one I was on, piloting it to the coast. With him was Mrs. Lindbergh. Later we met again, as we found ourselves houseguests in the same hospitable Los Angeles home. I think our hosts were no more surprised to have flying guests appear from Long Island than from Long Beach twenty miles away. For aviation has shrunk the continent to less than 12 hours of speed flying, or 36 hours by regular commercial planes.

In fact, so quickly do miles slip away for air travelers that those who are accustomed to thinking in terms of flying often startle their friends who do not. I know I often have to be "whereabouts unknown" for several hours in order not to worry people who are expecting me to arrive somewhere at a given hour.

An illustrative instance happened on a recent visit to the coast. I found one day that I had to make a speech at a dinner in a middle western city. My course by air from Los Angeles was about thirteen hundred miles each way. Of course I flew. The morning of the day of the dinner I was thirty-six hours away by train schedule from the well-known banquet chicken. I didn't dare let my hosts know where I was lest they despair of my arriving. As it was, I think I turned up a good two hours before my engagement.

It seems to me one of the most significant characteristics of the Lindberghs is their habit of doing everything together. Even on the first flight of the new orange-and-black airplane, Mrs. Lindbergh went aloft. She is a willing and capable crew on long flights. I have often heard the Colonel speak of the days when he flew alone and found difficulty in doing certain things. Now he increasingly counts on her active cooperation. One of her responsibilities is photographing; or she may take the controls when her husband is occupied with "shooting the sun," for instance. Indeed, when they made their transcontinental record of fourteen and three-quarters hours from coast to coast, Mrs. Lindbergh, using a sextant, acted as navigator. On the trip to the Orient, she added the duties of radio operator to these.

Both of these people consider flying a matter of routine. When they start across the continent, each of them usually takes but a single suitcase. The only *extras* they wear are parachutes. Mrs. Lindbergh has never had to use one of these life preservers of the air, but the Colonel has four times qualified for the mythical Caterpillar Club whose membership consists solely of individuals who have made an emergency jump.

About baggage. When I flew out to California that time (there have been many transcontinental crossings since), my secretary was with me. We took much work with us, planning to conduct an itinerant office as we went. Coming from the cold of the wintry east to the summer of California with six weeks before us, we naturally had a good deal of baggage. Actually with parachutes and emergency rations, I think the indecent total was thirteen pieces.

When we left for the return journey, Colonel Lindbergh saw this mountain of baggage piled high in the car.

"And what might that be?" he asked disapprovingly.

During our explanation, I sensed he was making a comparison with the impedimenta of a typical Lindbergh journey.

He turned to his wife with a grin. "Don't you get any foolish ideas from this," he admonished.

But I had a large plane in which I could easily carry half a ton so I didn't feel so guilty of violating any air tradition as I might.

In passing, I should like to say that pluck seems to me to be one of Mrs. Lindbergh's most dominant

characteristics. Under her gentleness lies a fine
courage to meet both physical and spiritual hazards
with understanding. In addition to the business of
the colonel's flying, the pair have used the air for
exploration, over sea and over jungle, and have had
the informal fun of "sitting down" in western desert places and making camp where they would.

For them, aviation is essentially not a "cause."
But being asked to do all kinds of things "for aviation," as if it were a charity or a patriotic duty, is
an old story for the Lindberghs. Important as aviation is in their lives, they cannot think of it in any
such light. It is a profession and a present reality
and quite as much a matter of fact as any other
twentieth-century development.

The first transport license issued to a woman
went to Phoebe Omlie. Mrs. Omlie started her
flying career in 1920 as a parachute jumper and
wing walker, breaking the women's altitude record
on July 10, 1921. Later, with her husband, Captain Omlie, a world war instructor who had had
eleven years of flying experience, she established
the largest flying school in the south, the Mid South
Airways at Memphis, Tennessee.

In the early years, Mrs. Omlie did considerable
flying instruction herself. Then one day a student
"froze" on the controls and she wasn't able to break
him loose.

Sometimes certain types of individuals become
rigid with· fear and hold so tightly to nearby objects that their grasp cannot be broken except by

knocking them unconscious. In a panic, a man may cling to the wheel of an automobile and go over a precipice unable to move a muscle. Or a drowning man fasten on his rescuer such an iron grip that both may be pulled under.

So in the old days, particularly before medical examinations were required, student pilots now and then reacted similarly. They held the controls so firmly that their instructors had no recourse but to hit them with whatever tool could be reached. To-day, there may be had a mechanically opening release which acts from the pilot's cockpit to disengage the dual controls if necessary. Then, the instructor kept with him a belaying pin of sorts for use in emergency.

Probably Mrs. Omlie was too small to reach her man in the front cockpit, and she had to sit helplessly waiting till they crashed. She still carries a scar from that accident and since then has done little or no primary instructing.

For years Mrs. Omlie has flown a Monocoupe for the company which manufactures them at Moline, Illinois. She is one of the best known pilots of this type of craft in the country, and with it has won races and established records. For this job she leaves her husband to carry on alone at Memphis for a few months each summer while she goes north.

A commercial side of the Omlie family's activities is crop dusting, an increasingly important phase of aeronautical work with agriculture. Especially in the south where much has to be done to combat the boll weevil in the cotton district, airplanes have been utilized to spray poison from the air.

Mrs. Omlie also showed her skill and unselfish courage in the Mississippi Valley flood disaster which did vast damage in the regions around Memphis. Medicines and Red Cross nurses were needed in the stricken area, but bridges were down and roads submerged. In this emergency Mrs. Omlie, using her plane, carried medical supplies and food rations to numberless sufferers. Today the Omlies are continuing with their school at Memphis and have, I believe, a sound and promising business.

Another couple I happen to know who are making a living together out of aviation are William and Frances Marsalis. They conduct a school at the New York Municipal Airport. Frances Marsalis, who is known as well by her own name of Harrell, has done as much exhibition flying as any other woman active today. She has toured the country with the Curtiss Exhibition Company, stunting and doing formation flying. And if students wish a woman instructor, Mrs. Marsalis takes them on. She is a sound flyer and an experienced one.

Then there are the O'Donnells, Gladys and Lloyd, of Long Beach, California, and the Haizlips in St. Louis.

Another air husband and wife combination is Louise and Herb Thaden. He was a flyer during the war and later was associated with a Pittsburgh

group which put out an all-metal plane that he designed. Later, he accepted a position in a technical
capacity with General Aviation, a General Motors
subsidiary which took over the Fokker interests.
Louise Thaden demonstrates her husband's planes
and ferries company officials about. At one time
she held the women's endurance record and, as I
have written, won the first derby. She held the office of National Secretary of the "99s" for two
years and is reckoned one of the ablest women
flyers.

Together she and I once carried out an interesting experiment showing the value of air transportation. A few weeks after her son was born, the
National Air Races were held in Chicago. Of
course, all pilots hope to be present wherever they
are, if only for one day. The doctor had forbidden
Mrs. Thaden to go.

"Why," he said, "do you think I would allow you
to jolt along in a train for eleven hours—and come
back worn out?"

"How about going by air?" his patient inquired:
"How long will it take?"

"Oh, about three or four hours."

"Well, if you let someone else fly and take it easy
—and come back in two days, I might consent."

Mrs. Thaden knew I was going from New York
so she telephoned and asked me to stop by Pittsburgh and pick her up. Of course, I did and we
made Chicago in three hours. The doctor admitted
the trip had done her no harm when she returned.

By the way, her son has had many hours in the air and he isn't yet two. But so have most of the young children of air families.

One of the most picturesque of present-day women flyers is diminutive Laura Ingalls. She started to learn to fly at an eastern field, as I understand, but the instructors there discouraged her. They tried, at least. But Miss Ingalls doesn't stay discouraged long. So she transferred her activities to another school and thence in due course emerged with a license.

Especially notable is her ability as an aerial acrobat. She established a feminine record for loops with 980 of them consecutively, doing it as an exhibition and receiving a dollar a loop. Later she tried barrel rolls and succeeded in making 714 of these which is the record for both sexes.

Some critics protest against such exhibitions. I myself cannot see what harm they do. Certainly their execution requires sturdy equipment and skill and determination on the part of the pilot. They may not point the way to progress in aviation but they demonstrate its possibilities. As for women's doing them, that probably will be necessary for some time—for contrary to legal precedent, they (women) are considered guilty of incompetence until proved otherwise.

TWENTIETH CENTURY PIONEERS

BEHIND modern women pilots stand another group who are the real pioneers. While comparatively few in number they must have had plenty of what my grandmother called "spirit". Their era was mostly from 1910 to 1919. Since then I believe all have abandoned any active flying, save one, perhaps, who keeps a current Department of Commerce license.

History seems to be running backward in this rambling account of mine. In the midst of going from the modern woman flyer to the decade before, I recall that there are still others who hopped into the air long before those I am now calling pioneers. I'll retreat a hundred years or more to the very, very first "Lady Aeronauts."

Although she never flew herself, I doubt if any American woman had a larger hand in making flying a fact than Katherine Wright, the sister of Orville and Wilbur Wright.

The first flight of heavier than air craft was carried out December 17, 1903, at Kill Devil Hills, North Carolina. The little machine used weighed 750 pounds and had a twelve horse power engine. If flew 852 feet in one minute. Wilbur Wright was the pilot and Orville his alter ego on the ground.

As acclaim for the achievement began to roll in

from all sides, Orville is quoted as saying, "When the world speaks of the Wrights, it must include our sister. Much of our effort has been inspired by her."

The Wright brothers had no college education, but the sons of a minister, they were well read and studious. While the boys had a job printing office and then a bicycle shop as their vocation (with aeronautics always an avocation), Katherine Wright acquired Latin and Greek. The money she earned as teacher in these subjects she turned over to her brothers so they might continue their aeronautical experiments which by this time occupied them to the exclusion of bread-and-butter business. So Katherine Wright helped pay for and actually helped build the first heavier than air plane ever flown.

The first woman to receive a license as a pilot was I believe the Baroness de la Roche of France. That was in 1910. Before she took up flying she had raced automobiles and was a well known figure on the track. In 1913, she received the famous Coupe Femina for a flight covering approximately 160 miles. This distance was made in about four hours' time—a good demonstration of airplane performance of her day.

In 1911 Harriett Quimby won the first license for women in the United States. She was a newspaper woman in Boston and at one time dramatic editor of Leslie's Weekly, then a flourishing periodical. She learned to fly at the Moisant school on

Long Island. The record shows that her instruction covered thirty-three lessons with a little more than four and a half hours in the air. Shortly after she soloed, the Moisant flyers went on a tour of Mexico and America, but Harriett Quimby chose other worlds to conquer.

In 1909 Bleriot had flown the English Channel for the first time, and the feat evidently appealed to Miss Quimby as a mark to shoot for. At all events, on April 12, 1912, she crossed the English Channel from Deal, England, to Epihen, France, in her Bleriot monoplane. Hers was the first crossing by a woman, and probably the most perilous heavier than air flight up to that time attempted by a feminine pilot.

On this flight Harriett Quimby had an experience in fog flying. When she took off the visibility near the ground was poor but for safety's sake she wanted to fly high. Therefore, she plowed through to sunlight on the top of a layer of clouds at 6000 feet. Fortunately she had a compass and by following it managed to reach the opposite shore without being able to see it on the way across.

In appraising this fine feminine feat it must be remembered the pilot had no parachute and none of the instruments known today. Besides such lack, her plane and engine were far inferior in many ways to those in the air today.

I have seen pictures showing Harriett Quimby as she dressed the day of that flight and on others too. Extraordinary clothes! There was as much

Harriet Quimby

Publicizing an early flyer

contrast between flying togs of that day and this as
there is between the planes themselves. Miss
Quimby's costume material was purple satin.
There were full bloomers reaching below the knee
with high laced shoes below. She wore a blouse
with long full sleeves and high collar buttoned tight
around her neck. Her headgear as pictured in the
old photographs resembles nothing so much as a
monk's cowl. Accessories were goggles and gaunt-
lets and a long leather coat for cold weather flying.

We're more fortunate in our clothing today. In
an open cockpit plane it is sensible and comfortable
to dress either in breeks of some sort or routine
sport clothing of the season. In closed planes, any
street costume will do, as there is no exposure.

Harriett Quimby was killed at a Boston air meet
on July 1, 1912. She was flying her Bleriot monoplane, one of the best performers of that day, but
exceedingly unstable. From all accounts balance
had to be maintained with a bag of sand placed at
a specific point in the machine when there was no
passenger. When there was, he or she had to sit
immovable. A shift of this center of gravity,
whether caused by the movement of the sand or
the living ballast, meant disaster.

Apparently such a shift occurred at Boston. A
Mr. Willard in charge of the meet flew with Harriett Quimby. Toward the end of the flight at an
altitude of two thousand feet he moved unduly, the
monoplane gave a sharp dip and apparently went
out of control. Willard's body flew into the air

followed a few seconds later by that of the woman pilot.

John Moisant was one of the early American pilots. Among other things he had flown the English Channel and prior to 1911 had brought over flying equipment to this country with which he established the Moisant International Aviators, Inc. As I have said, Harriett Quimby took her instruction at his school.

In 1911 John Moisant was killed flying at New Orleans. Shortly after that, Mathilde, his sister, learned to fly and started out with the survivors of the original Moisant touring group. With them in 1911 she went to Mexico in a series of flying exhibitions. There they narrowly escaped losing their equipment to the revolutionists and literally had to fly for their lives. Just a year after her brother's death Mathilde flew at New Orleans and there was presented with the cup which had been destined for him.

Accidents were sprinkled through these busy months. Finally, toward the close of 1912, she insisted on flying in unpromising weather at Wichita Falls, Texas, rather than disappoint a crowd which had waited several days for her. Landing in a high wind, she apparently bounced into the air again. In order to avoid injuring people who immediately rushed out on the field, she opened the throttle and tried to take off. She was only partly successful and landed again this time rolling over. Splinters of the broken propeller punctured the gas tanks and set the ship and pilot on fire. Mathilde was rescued with her hair and leggings singed.

Then in earnest did the Moisant family step in. They had previously urged their daughter to abandon flying and this time they succeeded in gaining their end. It is said the reward for parental obedience was a plantation in San Salvador. At all events, after five strenuous months, Mathilde Moisant ceased to fly.

Outstanding among the earlier women flyers was Ruth Law. She was born in Lynn, Massachusetts. She obtained the third license granted to women in America and I don't believe aviation has seen a more picturesque figure than this original Ruth. She went after flying with great determination. With her there was a real feeling of competition against the men of the day who in training and equipment were forging ahead of the few individual women struggling for a chance in the air.

Here is a story which gives a picture of the kind of thing Miss Law wanted to do and how she did it:

Early in November, 1916, Victor Carlstrom took off on what was to be an epoch-making flight. He started from Chicago hoping to reach New York, in an effort to establish a new non-stop distance record. No one had ever flown so far. Carlstrom flew a Jenny, the latest in military planes, and he carried the then very large load of 206 gallons of gasoline.

He had covered 452 miles when a fuel line broke and he had to come down at Erie, Pennsylvania.

In the meantime Ruth Law had been thinking about exactly the same flight. The plane she had was a Curtiss D pusher with a fuel capacity of 53 gallons.

So, a couple of weeks after Carlstrom's flight, she left Chicago. It was a gusty day and the pilot had a hard time getting the plane out of Grant Park. Even without her extra load of gasoline, that place offered a pretty restricted area. Once off, her troubles were not over for she had to skim along over the city at a 200 foot altitude, dodging in and out among the buildings, until she reached open country.

Profiting by Carlstrom's misfortune, Miss Law had installed a rubber hose as a fuel line, so that she would not be troubled with its breaking. Her instruments, in contrast to those used today, were a compass and a clock! However, because she hoped to make a record, she also carried a barograph to show she had not landed.

Her clothes for the flight consisted of "two layers of wool and two layers of leather." She chose the popular knickers of the day and a wool hockey cap. Even with this warm attire, it must have been bitterly cold stitting forward on the little machine entirely unprotected against the wind.

Nevertheless Ruth Law remained in the air for five hours and 45 minutes or until she had used her last drop of gasoline. She landed at Hornell, New York, 590 miles from Chicago and 128 miles beyond Erie.

Not having an airport handy, she came down in a farmyard. As she crawled stiffly from the seat, someone in the crowd which quickly gathered asked her if she had had any food since morning. She shook her head.

"I have to fix the plane before I can think about that," she said.

She thereupon busied herself tying her craft securely to a tree lest the wind injure it. When she was satisfied to leave, hospitable citizens took her to town where she dined on scrambled eggs, and thawed out.

The original plan had been to make her first stop at Binghamton. Fuel was ordered there and Curtiss mechanics from Hammondsport were waiting to service the plane. Consequently Miss Law took aboard only enough gasoline for the intervening distance and then hopped off. Arrived at Binghamton, she at first insisted on trying to push through that night. But in the face of darkness and none too promising weather, she reluctantly consented to stay where she was until the next morning.

Today it is simple to fly this short distance to New York. A sidelight on the difficulties encountered then, is Miss Law's experience in crossing New York City. About the time she reached the Harlem canal her motor began to sputter from lack of gas. Apparently, not wishing to carry any more weight than she had to, she had come from Binghamton with barely enough to reach her goal. The

tanks, of necessity, had been so placed that in order
to drain them entirely she had to rock the plane and
splash fuel into the carburetor. Bobbing along
thus, she reached the vicinity of Twenty-third
Street when the motor began to give more trouble
than ever. She used the last of her fuel to gain altitude and then with a dead stick glided to a predetermined landing spot on Governor's Island.

What a welcome she received! General Leonard
Wood greeted her and bands played and flags flew.
She was given the Aero Club Medal of Merit and
$2500. The great explorers Amundsen and Peary
were among those who acclaimed her, as did also
very generously, Victor Carlstrom whom she had
vanquished.

The following years for Ruth Law were filled
with all kinds of activities, including barnstorming.
One colorful incident stands out particularly. Until 1916, the statue of Liberty was lighted only by
the electric bulbs in the lifted torch. The New
York *World* waged a successful campaign to have
the whole figure adequately illuminated. President
Wilson and Ruth Law were the headliners on the
first night of the new lights. He was to press the
button to turn them on and she was to fly as a
feature. The performance went off as scheduled,
with Miss Law appearing out of the darkness carrying magnesium flares on her wing tips and the
word "Liberty" in electric lights on the under surface.

After a few years of barnstorming during which

she did aerial acrobatics, Miss Law retired with her husband to California where she now lives.

Whenever famous names in aviation are mentioned, "Stinson" is among them. While there were two brothers in the family who entered the ranks of aviation, I shall confine myself to the sisters, Marjorie and Katherine. I could not begin to enumerate all the incidents in the career of either one, so I shall tell only a few tales of each.

Let's take Katherine first. She obtained her license in 1912 and devoted a few years afterward to exhibition flights here and abroad. From what I can learn she received recognition and medals of honor everywhere for her exploits. One of the most interesting flights she made was in 1917. She, like Ruth Law, had tried to enter the Government flying service and had been turned down. However, she was able to borrow a ship from the army to use on a special mission for the Red Cross. It was a "Jenny" and a new type to her but she soloed it after fifteen minutes' dual flight.

Bearing formal notice to Secretary McAdoo that Buffalo had oversubscribed its quota, she set out one afternoon from that city for Washington, D. C. Her first stop was Syracuse and then Albany where she landed on Van Rensselaer Island in the Hudson River. She stayed in Albany all night and resumed her journey in the morning.

Her navigating aids were noteworthy. She had a map from Buffalo to Albany, but from there she followed the New York Central tracks to reach

New York, her next stopping place. To Philadelphia and Washington she used simply a Pennsylvania Railroad folder as a guide! As she passed
various cities, she threw out Red Cross literature
and circled over them, so that it was late in the
evening of the second day when she came down in
Washington on the Polo Grounds.

The pictures of Katherine Stinson show her in
what looks like a ready made jacket suit, with a
curl over her shoulder and a ribbon on her hair.
Probably as difficult as flying the 373 miles in a
single day was keeping that curl and ribbon in
place. At the time of this trip, the pilot weighed
105 pounds and had to stand up in the cockpit to
enable the crowd to see her.

Another flight worth remembering was that when
she bettered Ruth Law's distance record. She
started out from Chicago under entirely different
auspices from her predecessor. Before leaving she
was sworn in as a postal clerk and carried a sack
of mail containing sixty-one special letters. She,
too, left from Grant Park and followed the identical
route of her feminine rival. However, she not only
sailed by Erie, but Hornell as well and landed in
Binghamton, establishing a new long distance record of 783 miles and one for endurance, too, with
ten hours in the air.

On the *Friendship* flight I have said the crew
was supplied with malted milk tablets. When I
took them I had no idea that Miss Stinson had set
the precedent, but in accounts of this flight of hers,

she says, "I took three handfuls of malted milk tablets, one for each meal."

Unlike Miss Law, Katherine Stinson encountered trouble in landing. In deep mud, she nosed over and broke her propeller. Twice she repeated the performance in the week following, owing to the inadequacy of the field from which she was trying to take off. But she made New York eventually and landed at a field on Sheepshead Bay.

Cross country trips of the simplest kind were unusual and dangerous experiences before 1920. In fact, it was generally the custom to ship airplanes by rail from place to place for the exhibitions which were the order of the day. From this fact one can get a measure of Katherine Stinson's performance in the days when airplanes were never thought of as transportation means.

Two years after Katherine had soloed, Marjorie decided to fly. She was not quite eighteen when she presented herself at the Wright Brothers school in Dayton in June, 1914.

One of the Wright brothers looked over the youthful aspirant. "I'm sorry we can't accept you until your parents wire their consent", said he. If we can judge by Miss Stinson's own account of the incident, we can visualize a very angry little figure facing Mr. Wright. She confesses she had on her longest skirt, yet here was a man refusing the money she had brought for her instruction and really treating her as if she were a child.

After vigorously protesting, she consented to

telegraph her father and mother in San Antonio
for their formal permission. When it came, she
was permitted to enroll as a bona fide student.
With her were four others to be joined by a fifth
later on. Of course, they were men.

The plane the students used had a thirty horse
power motor in it and was in several respects different from the other models of the day. However,
it was like them in that it was a somewhat delicate
creature and could only be flown under the best conditions. Consequently flying instruction was in
force at dawn when the weather conditions were
likely to be most favorable. Marjorie Stinson
writes of these days that she sometimes managed
to get in five minutes in the morning and if she was
lucky five minutes again in the evening.

At that rate it took her six weeks to master her
course well enough to solo. During that period
she had many adventures. Apparently the class
went out en masse and captured the horses in a
neighboring pasture. They fished and flew kites
and waited hours around the field for chances to
fly.

Katherine Stinson visited her sister several times
to be sure she was progressing properly. On the
day before her first solo she paid an extra special
visit.

Like other flyers of her day whose income came
from teaching or giving exhibition flights—Marjorie Stinson spent the next few years flying here
and there about the country.

In 1917 she received a telegram from four Canadians asking her to train them in order that they might enter the air service of their country. The first four were followed by others and still others. In all she trained several score, not including chance civilians. One of her first difficulties during these intensive days was a requirement of the Canadians that they be taught the "three-in-one" method. That meant she had to change her ship from a wing warping type to one with ailerons. Instead of the three levers with which it was equipped, she had to work out means of substituting one operated by an automobile steering wheel. By the combined efforts of her pupils, her mechanic and herself that engineering feat was accomplished and she flight tested the machine.

With all her students she had to make an agreement that at a given signal they would release the controls to her, if she wished. This she did to overcome the handicap of her size. Being so much smaller than the individuals she was teaching, she might otherwise have been unable to manoeuver the plane in an emergency against their superior strength.

Today Marjorie Stinson is the only woman of this period who keeps an active Department of Commerce license.

THE FIRST WOMEN AERONAUTS

FEW people realize that more than a hundred years before the twentieth century pioneers, there were other women aeronauts. They did their flying in balloons.

In 1783, the first human being went aloft in a hot air paper bag invented by the Montgolfier brothers after long experimentation. A year later the first ascent by a woman was made at Lyons. From that time on, various feminine passengers braved the air until finally in 1799 the first woman soloed. She was Jeanne Genieve Garnerin who was the wife of Andre Jacques Garnerin, one of the greatest balloonists of the era. He and she subsequently added to their reputations by numerous other flights.

So proficient were the Garnerins that they held the title of Official aeronauts to Napoleon. When a fluke of fortune deprived them of this position, they originated soirées where ascensions were the feature of the occasion and for many years kept this form of entertainment popular.

The fluke of fortune of which I speak occurred at the Coronation of Napoleon in Paris, December 5, 1804. The Garnerins had been given charge of the aerial display of this great celebration. Besides other acts they planned to release numerous balloons of different sizes and kinds and shapes and colors. But their chef-d'oeuvre was a monster round envelope to which was attached a large gilded crown with colored lanterns hung on it in honor of the Empire.

When this special piece took the air a malevolent wind caught and carried it straight to Rome where with uncanny aim it found the tomb of Nero. The crown, originally planned as a mark of homage for the living Emperor was torn off and left hanging in jaunty abandon on the monument of one long dead. The balloon itself, after this prank, drifted over Lake Bracciano and was recovered intact.

This incident gave the Italian newspapers a far-fetched opportunity to be insulted. Consequently they vented their spleen against the French by publishing a few choice similes about Nero and Napoleon. Under the circumstances, Citizen Garnerin and his wife had to be released from official connection with the Emperor's air activities.

But it *is* an ill wind that blows nobody good. The person who stepped into the position vacated by the Garnerins was an altogether suitable successor. A beautiful and brilliant woman, Madame Blanchard was the next incumbent. She was inducted into office with great ceremony in 1810 as Napoleon's chief of air service. She was the widow of the balloonist Jean Pierre Blanchard who had been killed in an accident three years before. After his death, she carried on until she herself became as well known in France and neighboring countries as he had been.

Truly she must have been an unusual person for she combined rugged character and physique with the charming and delicate exterior demanded of femininity in that period. In the descriptions of her numerous flights, one is impressed with her showmanship, her good sense, and her originality. She had pluck, too, for she often stayed aloft all night in her fragile craft and made descents when morning gave her light.

Of course, the duties of a chief of air service were entirely different from those we impute to that office today. Then, whatever balloon the chief happened to have constituted the air force. There was no thought of aerial transportation as such. An ascent was a daring commercial spectacle or a social event. Madame Blanchard appeared at affairs where she was bidden by royal command and also carried on some exploits of her own when not needed at the palace fêtes.

With Napoleon's banishment, Madame Blanchard took up royal aeronauting for Louis XVIII. Her office under both rulers lasted until her tragic death in 1819.

On this occasion, Madame Blanchard planned one of the most spectacular ascents of her career. Except in the very earliest experiments hydrogen had been used to inflate the envelopes of all sized balloons. Despite knowledge that this gas was extremely inflammable, it had been the custom more and more frequently to make night ascents with a display of fireworks lighted on the ground just be-

fore the take off. Madame Blanchard had an extra
large framework hung on the outside of her basket
to hold her assortment. Inside her basket she had
a special lighted taper and bomb which she was to
set off when she reached a predetermined altitude.

Apparently there was a leak in the gas-bag over
her head, for as she picked up the taper a flame
shot from it and up the side of the ballon. A moment afterward her craft began to descend, blazing,
to earth. Chronicles of the day agree she landed
on a house, but differ as to whether she died from
burns or because of a fall from the roof to the
street.

La Blanchard is often spoken of as a martyr in
the advancement of lighter than air achievements.
Her death ended a specific military office in
France until balloons found use for observation
purposes in the siege of Paris in 1871.

The next important name the nineteenth century
gives us among women balloonists is not a new one.
The family of Garnerin again comes to the fore
in the person of Elisa, a niece of the original André
Jacques. She stands out from the other aeronauts
of the day because she undertook to make parachute descents. She went aloft sitting in a little
basket attached to a parachute which in turn hung
from one balloon. When the moment came to cut
off, she released a rope and settled earthward,
where she willed.

Possessed of a good deal of energy, she toured
Europe extensively, giving her special exhibitions.

She was in demand at marriages, soirées, pageants and king's coronations. She received besides lucrative offers to perform before crowds of city or country folk who collected to watch whatever she did. Her work seems more analogous to the barnstorming era in heavier than air craft than that of her contemporaries. And it is pleasant indeed to record that Elisa Garnerin, after making innumerable jumps and ascents, lived to a ripe old age and died peacefully in her bed.

England produced the next well known woman balloonist. Her name was Margaret Graham, and she was as different from Madame Blanchard or Mlle. Garnerin as anyone possibly could be. In the first place, she combined domesticity and a career in a more than modern manner. She was the mother of seven children and she managed to make exhibitions over all England and keep her home in London going at the same time.

Like Elisa Garnerin, she had advanced barnstorming ideas. She took passengers in her balloon and made them pay dearly for the experience. Her husband seems to have managed her business affairs and was almost always on hand when she performed. Now and then he even went aloft with her.

Mrs. Graham had a keen advertising sense. As she was definitely earning her living by her performances, she took to writing accounts of her exploits for the newspapers of the day. As can be imagined, these sometimes differed from what eye-

Madame Blanchard, famous pioneer

A pioneer aircraft factory

witnesses claimed—especially when reports of accidents were made. For Mrs. Graham had her share of mishaps.

Once she landed in the sea off Plymouth when a strong wind bore her away from shore. Another time she had the misfortune to displace with her dangling grappling hook a piece of stone coping which fell to the street and killed a pedestrian. Again, in a much too speedy descent, doubtless caused by lack of knowledge of the laws of expanding gases, she bumped herself into unconsciousness for six days. After a slow recovery, her determination and energy asserted themselves and she went on with her ballooning again.

Mrs. Graham preferred to begin her exhibitions in courtyards or tea gardens or other similarly enclosed places where the crowd could be kept at bay. Then, too, there she could often collect a modest fee from the curious ones who wished to get a near view of the craft before it went up. In an open space this was difficult to do as all showmen know.

In Mrs. Graham's time, as before, there was a great deal of interesting preparation before each flight. The hydrogen for the balloons which used that gas for buoyancy had to be made on the spot. Barrels of acid and old iron were set to bubbling for the populace to gape at and the precious gas generated, was visibly piped to the limp balloon.

As it filled and took shape, everyone became more and more excited.

Mrs. Graham was one of the first to use illumi-

nating gas for her lifting agent. She bought it
from the local gas works and often found the pressure so low that it took hours to fill the envelope
sufficiently. Sometimes, despite precautions, her
flights were considerably delayed from this cause.

"Personal appearances" were to Mrs. Graham
highly desirable. Not only were her ascents played
up, but she attempted to return out of the mysterious ether to the same spot to show herself again
during a given entertainment. I do not mean she
came back in her balloon. Oh, no. She brought
that down as best she could, wherever she could,
and left it to be guarded while she departed for the
rest of the show. Her second appearance before
the crowd who had seen her depart a while earlier
was the signal for a tremendous ovation with usually a few words from her in order.

Her program was well planned. Even though
she wished to get down and back to her "public"
as quickly as possible, she was careful that no spectators saw her preparations to land. At night she
waited until darkness hid her from their view and
in the daytime until she had passed beyond their
vision, either by high flying or low. Then she came
down as expeditiously as possible and anchored
just above the tree tops.

Her husband, in the meantime, had set forth in
a postchaise and had followed, as nearly as he could,
her course. He usually found her by sighting her
bobbing balloon twenty or thirty feet above the
roadway. He helped her down and escorted her

back for the expected grand climax of reappear-
ance.

A longer span of activity than is allowed to most
was Mrs. Graham's privilege. She continued to
make ascents for *forty* years and lived to see the
heyday and decline of her kind of ballooning.

I have said little concerning the clothes of "The
Only Female Aeronaut" of Victoria's reign, as
Mrs. Graham called herself. It is easy to see that
ballooning offered to her and her sisters limitless
scope for the use of all kinds of furbelows. Not
only was the person of the aeronaut decorated but
the craft as well. The beplumed and beribboned
equipages were designed to harmonize with and en-
hance the appearances of the performers. And
vice versa. The silks and satins of the day carried
right over into the very business of ballooning. It
seems almost as if the spectacular side of aerial
entertainment has never reached so high a pinnacle
as it did during this fabulous period of balloon
pageantry.

AIR TRAILS OF THE FUTURE

THERE is a mighty difference between the bedecked balloons of the eighteen hundreds and aircraft of today. The vehicles have altered so much in design and usage that aeronauts of a century ago, were they to revisit the earth, would recognize few familiar features in modern aeronautical activity. What will be the steps in the next hundred years? Will the distance covered be as great as that in the last?

Of course, it is more than futile to make prophecies—aviation ones especially. They usually turn out more or less like the famous pronouncement of the sour and distinguished scientists long ago. They declared, you remember (and proved mathematically), that a heavier than air machine, capable of lifting itself off the earth could never, never be built.

I can remember being told as late as 1924 that air cooled radial motors of more than 60 h.p. would never be successful. Now practically all motors on commercial aircraft are this type and some of them develop more than 600 h.p. I can also remember hearing it said that commercial flying at night would prove an impossibility. The United States now maintains 17,500 miles of lighted airways over which 63,000 miles are scheduled daily between sundown and sunup.

But prophesying has two sides.

To show how rapidly some predictions are fulfilled, I recall a conversation I heard the other day. A woman reporter and a man who had been a pilot in the World War were discussing modern air transport. The ex-flyer had just alighted from a big airliner and was describing how tea had been served.

"A table cloth, and cups and spoons," I heard him say. "If anyone had told me in 1918 that people would ever sit calmly in airplanes and drink tea, I would have laughed my head off."

His companion was amused.

"How do you suppose air travel will improve in the next ten years?", she asked.

"Oh, mostly through refinements of what we have now, I think", he answered. "It will probably be as commonplace to use planes then as to ride on trains now. No one will get any kick out of flying—except old timers who remember."

"Your prophecies are not exciting enough", the reporter said. "Can't you do better?"

"I'm not sure what you mean."

"Well, just this. Maybe the airplane of the future will look very much like the ones we have today. Maybe just by gradually improved design and improved motors and improved what not, it will reach its ultimate perfection. A good many of aviation's leaders think so, I know. But isn't there always the chance that some obscure investigator will stumble on an entirely new principle, and by applying it, make obsolete in a day what we think pretty O.K. now? Such an event would be exciting and that's what I want to hear about."

Most people, I thought, are like the reporter. They want startlers. And what's more, they are likeliest to believe the ones which appear most impossible.

I told a group of not very progressive women once that within two years everyone present would have been in an airplane, i.e., anyone who traveled at all. A good many heads shook negatively to that. But when I described the possibility of future high altitude flying in planes sealed to protect passengers in the rarefied air, going at speeds of 500 to 1000 m.p.h., they took such a development almost for granted.

Yet I maintain my prophecy that aviation, as we know it today, will be accepted as an everyday means of locomotion before we progress to stratosphere flying.

After all, when one considers it, the simple idea of flying from one place to another, is a real startler. What would the early balloonists have thought of doing this? They went up for sport, for acclaim or for reward, and then came down—where it didn't matter. To go by air to a predetermined destination was never attempted.

But the world today has the transportation idea firmly fixed. It even invades sport flying, which as often as not, means going by airplane several hundred miles (instead of thirty by automobile) for a game of golf.

So propnecies, I think, should follow this lead, because it seems probable that actual development will. If so, increasing speed will be of paramount importance. Aviation has nothing much to sell unless it be this. Today the world's record is more than 400 miles an hour, attained in a specially built racer. But already there are some commercial airlines in the United States which use airplanes capable of more than 200 miles an hour. Certainly it will not be long before this speed is a general thing —and higher and higher ones will be reached in sporting events.

A physician has recently completed tests which show that apparently the human body can travel up to 700 miles an hour and beyond with no ill effects. Such word is encouraging if I am right in believing the inhabitants of this planet want and will attain increasingly greater speeds as time goes on.

Already several gentlemen are trying to think out ways and means of accommodating. I can tell you of one who has reached the point of considering airplanes projectiles. Beyond certain speeds the wings of a plane tend to retard forward motion. He proposes to design retractable wings which can be operated by the pilot. If it is desired to go very fast, the wings would be pulled in. In landing, or taking off, or just cruising along, they would be spread for needed lift. Of course, this is in addition to pulling in the landing gear, as done on some types now.

Other inventors are working on rocket planes in various parts of the world. Some of these are being developed solely to find a substitute for conventional power plants. Others have behind them enthusiasts who seek to travel to far places, with the moon as a favorite location.

Of course such projects have more than the problem of attaining speed to solve. Such craft, like the stratosphere plane which I have mentioned before, have to be very strong and sealed to protect human life. A supply of oxygen for the journey must be taken along far beyond the "seven mile limit" where the air is not dense enough for earth beings to breathe. Only once,—so far—has the stratosphere been penetrated. That was in the flight of August Piccard and Paul Kitsen, who last year reached a height of 51,775 ft. in a special metal sphere attached to a balloon.

Of as much interest as speed, seem to be airplanes of gigantic size. No sooner had the DO-X been built to carry 162 passengers than plans for a flying boat double its size were announced by another concern. What the physical limits of these Gargantuan monsters are I do not know. If there aren't any, perhaps their measure of usefulness will decide their proportions. So far, large units have not proved profitable in air line operation, and the shadow of economics always hovers above any development.

Every week one can read of proposed tailless planes, wingless planes, motorless planes, and even

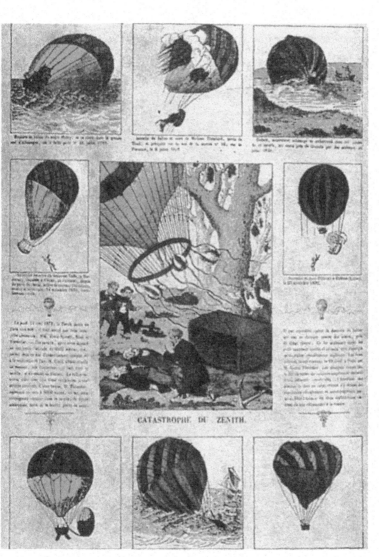

CATASTROPHE DU ZÉNITH.

An artist's warning to early aeronauts

No fete was complete without its aeronaut

pilotless planes, where a mechanical robot takes the place of the human equation. Pictures appear of planes that can land equally well on ice or snow or water or land. For the man who suggested what flyers really needed was a plane that could land on a tree or a house, there are proposed safety devices for nice "comings down" including plane 'chutes.

Steam engines, gasoline engines, fuel oil engines —prophecies concerning each may be had for the asking. Less exciting perhaps than some others are those of improvements in instruments and radio beams to guide the pilot through any weather to his home port, be that a concrete island anchored in the middle of the ocean or a plot near the city— crying to be perfected and put into universal use.

What about trans-atlantic flying? Of course that will come—and, according to good reports, sooner than most people believe. So will going around the world the other way, from pole to pole. In fact, it looks as if airplanes will pretty well cover the earth, in the words of one of our best known advertisements.

And perhaps contrary to what has always been the case, i.e. that increased speed has resulted in increased cost, aviation may prove one of the cheapest forms of transportation. From ox-cart to automobile, expense has mounted with m.p.h.'s. Would it not be pleasant, indeed, to have the process reversed?

If this prophecy is fulfilled, railroads take warn-

ing! Put wings on your box-cars or buy a control-
ling interest in the right air-line.

I have one more word for this prophecy chapter.
That is the simple reminder that the startling developments people like are only possible through
wide-spread labor in many fields. The ex-war pilot
was right. Even a new discovery is just fitting in,
in the jig-saw puzzle of scientific achievement, an
unusually large piece. Many little curley-kews are
needed around it to make its meaning clear. All
kinds of minds in all kinds of schools and labora-
tories, or alone in cubby-holes, are trying to work
out theoretical details of efficient flight. Helping
them are those who put the theories to practical
use. That women will share in these endeavors,
even more than they have in the past, is my wish—
and prophecy.

ACROSS THE ATLANTIC—SOLO

London, May 25, 1932

ACTIVE preparation for the Atlantic Flight started after I had finished the manuscript of "The Fun Of It." Indeed, the book itself was finished by the time I left New York . . . Here, at the request of the publishers, is a final chapter describing the flight itself—a postscript from overseas.

Starting from Harbor Grace, Newfoundland, on the afternoon of May 20, 1932, I landed near Londonderry in the north of Ireland the next morning, thirteen and a half hours after the take-off. That, briefly, is the story of my solo flight across the Atlantic.

Ever since my first crossing in the "Friendship," in 1928 when I was merely a passenger, I have wanted to attempt a solo flight. Then, a few months ago I decided upon it seriously. My Lockheed-Vega plane, which had been under charter to a transport line at Washington, was free. I found that Bernt Balchen was ready to take charge of its re-conditioning, while my husband, always a good sport about my flying activities, was ready to back the plan with full enthusiasm. For several reasons it seemed wise not to talk about the proposed flight in advance. After all, there was nothing to talk about until it became an actuality, and from the start I definitely planned that I might abandon it at any time.

It was clear in my mind that I was undertaking the flight because I loved flying. I chose to fly the Atlantic because I wanted to. It was, in a measure, a self-justification—a proving to me, and to anyone else interested, that a woman with adequate experience could do it.

The plane was taken to Teterboro Airport in New Jersey just across the Hudson from New York. There is located the now unused Fokker plant, and close by lived Bernt Balchen, who with his wife are close friends of Mr. Putnam and mine. Bernt of course is one of the very finest flyers living, and also a great technician with rare engineering training. He has the happy characteristic of conservatism and being unhurried in his judgments. At the outset we told Bernt that if at any time he thought I couldn't do it, or the ship couldn't do it, I would abandon it, and no harm done. But Bernt never once wavered in his confidence, and that confidence helped immeasurably in sustaining my own.

First Balchen and his helpers strengthened the fuselage of the Lockheed which had had some hard knocks in the three years I have flown it. Then extra fuel tanks were put in the wings and a large tank installed in the cabin. These increased the fuel capacity to 420 gallons, giving the plane a cruising radius of about 3200 miles.* In addition, there was tankage for 20 gallons of oil. Loaded, the plane weighed about 5500 pounds.

Additional instruments were installed, including a drift indicator and additional compasses. Of the latter I had three—an aperiodic, a magnetic and a directional gyro, for checking one against the other.

From Pratt & Whitney in Hartford I secured a new "Wasp" motor, for my old one had flown a bit too long for the Atlantic grind. This was a supercharged engine developing 500 horsepower which behaved magnificently under grueling conditions. As important as the motor is its fuel and oil, and under the guidance of Major Edwin Aldrin, an accomplished flyer, my tanks were filled at Teterboro, and later at St. John and Harbor Grace, with Stanavo gasoline and oil.

During this time of preparation the plane was chartered to Bernt Balchen, who was actively working with Lincoln Ellsworth in preparation for a South Polar flight. Ellsworth was having another plane built on the Pacific Coast and it was taken for granted that Balchen was making tests with mine with the possibility of including it also

* Ed. note: On the course Miss Earhart flew the shortest distance from Harbor Grace to the Irish coast was 1,860 miles. The distance she actually flew was 2,026½ miles, and the distance from Harbor Grace to Paris 2,640 miles.

in their Antarctic program. In the meanwhile, as
opportunity offered, I would drive over from my
home at Rye and get in odd hours in the air. Most
of these were devoted to blind flying until I felt
really confident of my ability to handle the ship
without looking outside of the cockpit—that is,
flying it solely with instruments.

As May moved on we studied the weather maps
with increasing interest. As usual with all flight
projects, Dr. James H. Kimball in the New York
office of the United States Weather Bureau was
of the greatest assistance. We never talked definitely of my plans and I don't know that he was
aware exactly what was up until the last moment.
He was, as always, tireless in his co-operation.

On the afternoon of the eighteenth of May, the
weather map was anything but promising. A per-
sistent "low" with its inevitable bad weather hung
over the eastern Atlantic. It seemed probable that
many days might elapse before a promising break
would come. Much as I wanted to move up to
Harbor Grace to be ready, I was almost resigned
to further days of waiting.

On Friday, the twentieth, my husband went to
town and later in the morning I drove to Teterboro to talk things over with Bernt and do a little
flying. The ship by then was ready to go. I arrived about 11:30. Eddie Gorski, our mechanic at
the hangar, told me there was a telephone call. It
was my husband, at Dr. Kimball's office. They
had just gone over the morning weather reports,

from ships at sea, from England and from the key
stations of the United States.

"And how is it from here to Harbor Grace?"
I asked.

"Perfect. Fine visibility all the way."

That settled it.

"We'll go this afternoon," I told my husband.
"I'll see Bernt and will get off as soon as possible."

Ten minutes later, after Bernt and I had talked,
I called back and told Mr. Putnam that we
planned to start at three. For me there wasn't
time for luncheon. Instead I drove back to Rye
as fast as I could. There I changed into jodphurs
and windbreaker, gathered up my leather flying
suit, maps and a few odds and ends and raced back
to the field.

I reached the field at 2:55. At 3:15 we took
off. Three hours and thirty minutes later we were
at St. John, New Brunswick. Early the next
morning we flew to Harbor Grace in Newfoundland arriving at 2:15 P.M. There detailed
weather reports from Mr. Putnam awaited us.
The outlook wasn't perfect but it was promising.
I had planned to leave Harbor Grace in the evening. Thus by the time night came the load would
be lightened somewhat while I would still be fresh
for night flying.

Bernt had flown the plane to Harbor Grace
while I rested in the fuselage behind the extra tank,
with Eddie Gorski beside me. So, the start decided, I left Bernt and Eddie checking ship and

motor while I found a friendly bed and restful nap.
In ample time I was awakened. The later telegrams confirmed our decision. At the field, the
engine was warmed up. A final message from my
husband was handed to me. I shook hands with
Bernt and Eddie, and climbed into the cockpit.
The southwest wind was nearly right for the runway. At twelve minutes after seven, I gave her
the gun. The plane gathered speed, and despite
the heavy load rose easily.

A minute later I was headed out to sea.

For several hours there was fair weather with a
lingering sunset. And then the moon came up over
a low bank of clouds. For those first hours I was
flying about 12,000 feet. And then something
happened that has never occurred in my twelve
years of flying. The altimeter, the instrument
which records height above ground, failed. Suddenly the hands swung around the dial uselessly
and I knew the instrument was out of commission
for the rest of the flight.

About 11:30, the moon disappeared behind some
clouds, and I ran into rather a severe storm with
lightning, and I was considerably buffeted about,
and with difficulty held my course. In fact, I probably got off my course at this point to some extent
because it was very rough. This lasted for at least
an hour. Then I flew on in calmer weather though
in the midst of clouds. Once I saw the moon for
a fleeting instant and thought I could pull out on
top of the clouds, so I climbed for half an hour

when suddenly I realized I was picking up ice.

I knew by the climb of the ship which was not as fast as usual that it was accumulating a weight of ice. Then I saw slush on the windowpane. In addition, ice began to coat my air speed indicator so that it refused to register accurately on the panel before me.

In such a situation one has to get into warmer air, so I went down hoping the ice would melt. I descended until I could see the waves breaking although I could not tell exactly how far I was above them. I kept flying here until fog came down so low that I dared not keep on at such an altitude. Instrument-flying cannot be done safely very near the surface with the equipment we have today.

There was nothing left but to seek a middle ground, that is, to fly under the altitude at which I picked up ice and over the water by a sufficient margin. This would have been much easier to do had I been able to know my height.

Later, I tried going up again with the same result. So I gave up, just plowing through the "soup" and not looking out of the cockpit again until morning came. I depended on the instruments there to tell me the position of the plane in space, as under these conditions human faculties fail. Had I not been equipped with the best I could never have succeeded. The directional gyro, which is freest of all from fluctuations if set every 15 minutes, was a real life-saver.

About four hours out of Newfoundland, I noticed a small blue flame licking through a broken weld in the manifold ring. I knew that it would grow worse as the night wore on. However, the metal was very heavy and I hoped it would last until I reached land. I was indeed sorry that I had looked at the break at all because the flames appeared so much worse at night than they did in the daytime.

As daylight dawned, I found myself between two layers of clouds, the first very high, probably twenty thousand feet, the lower ones little fluffy white clouds near the water. This was the first sight of the sea in daylight.

I noticed from the white caps that there was a northwest wind. The little white clouds soon grew packed and resembled a vast snow field. I could see on the leading edge of my wings particles of ice which had not yet melted. Soon I went a little higher and ran into another bank of clouds. I was in these for at least an hour and then came out in a clear space again over the white snow fields.

By this time, the upper layer was thin enough for the sun to come through, and it was as dazzling as on real snow. I had dark glasses but it was too much for me even so, and I came down through the lower layer to fly in the shade, as it were.

Anyway, ten hours had passed, and I wished to see the water lest I was passing a boat. I had seen one vessel shortly after I left Harbor Grace. I blinked my navigation lights but apparently no one saw me as I was flying high. Then I picked up either a fishing vessel or an oil tanker off the coast of Ireland, but those were the only two I saw until I met a fleet near the coast.

From then on I met sunshine and low hanging clouds, most of which I kept under even though they were very near the water.

By the way, I didn't bother much about food for myself. The really important thing was fuel for the engine. It drank more than 300 gallons of gasoline. My own trans-Atlantic rations consisted of one can of tomato juice which I punctured and sipped through a straw.

Of course, the last two hours were the hardest. My exhaust manifold was vibrating very badly, and then I turned on the reserve tanks and found the gauge leaking. I decided I should come down at the very nearest place, wherever it was. I had flown a set compass course all night. Now I changed to due east and decided to head for Ireland. I did not wish to miss the tip of Ireland and the weather was such I couldn't see very far. I thought I must be south of the course, for I had been told by the weather man in New York that I might find rain in that direction. When I ran into the storm I thought therefore I probably was in this "weather" he anticipated. Then when breaking white caps below disclosed a wind from the northwest

I was sure I must be south. As it happened, I probably was exactly on my course, and I think I hit Ireland about the middle.

I started down the coast and found thunderstorms lower in the hills. Not having the altimeter and not knowing the country, I was afraid to plow through those lest I hit one of the mountains, so I turned north where the weather seemed to be better and soon came across a railroad which I followed hoping it would lead me to a city, where there might be an airport.

The first place I encountered was Londonderry, and I circled it hoping to locate a landing field but found lovely pastures instead. I succeeded in frightening all the cattle in the county, I think, as I came down low several times before finally landing in a long, sloping meadow. I couldn't have asked for better landing facilities, as far as that is concerned.

There ended the flight and my happy adventure. Beyond it lay further adventures of hospitality and kindness at the hands of my friends in England, France, Italy, Belgium and America.

Aviation Books by Women

Bacon, Gertrude. Memories of Land and Sky. London, Methuen, 1928.

Barry, Mary Elizabeth and Hanna, Paul R. Wonder Flights of Long Ago. New York, Appleton, 1930.

Beale, Marie. Modern Magic Carpet. Baltimore, J. H. Furst, 1930.

Camac, Harriett. From India to England by Air. Privately printed, 1930.

De Sibour, Violette. Flying Gypsies. New York, Putnam, 1930.

Earhart, Amelia. "20 hrs. 40 min." New York, Putnam, 1930.

Goldsmith, Margaret. Zeppelin, A Biography. New York, Morrow, 1931.

Gray, Jack Stearns. Up. Strasburg, Va., Shenandoah Press, 1931.

Heath, Lady Mary and Wolfe, Stella Murray. Woman and Flying. London, Long, 1929.

Jacobs, Anne Marguerite. Knights of the Wing. New York, Century, 1928.

Ovington, Adelaide. An Aviator's Wife. New York, Dodd, Mead, 1920.

Verrill, Dorothy. Sky Girl. New York, Century, 1930.

—— Aircraft Book for Boys. New York, Harper, 1930.